TOUGH WOMEN

ADVENTURE STORIES

Stories of grit, courage and determination

Featuring stories by

Sarah Outen • Anna McNuff • Emily Chappell •
Emma Svensson • Ann Daniels • Anoushé Husain •
Antonia Bolingbroke-Kent • Rea Kolbl • Rickie Cotter •
Kate Rawles • Annie Lloyd-Evans • Vedangi Kulkarni

EDITED BY JENNY TOUGH

summersd

An Hachette UK Company
www.hachette.co.uk

Summersdale Publishers Ltd
Part of Octopus Publishing Group Limited
Carmelite House
50 Victoria Embankment
LONDON
EC4Y 0DZ
UK

www.summersdale.com

Printed and bound by CPI Group (UK) Ltd, Croydon, CR0 4YY

ISBN: 978-1-78783-300-5

Substantial discounts on bulk quantities of Summersdale books are available to corporations, professional associations and other organizations. For details contact general enquiries: telephone: +44 (0) 1243 771107 or email: enquiries@summersdale.com.

You're tougher than you think

CONTENTS

Foreword **Jenny Tough**..4

Wild at Heart **Aliénor le Gouvello**.............................14

Modern-Day Explorer **Ann Daniels**......................28

Mango Happy **Anna McNuff**.................................48

Where the Musk Oxen Roam **Annie Lloyd-Evans** 60

Why Me? **Anoushé Husain**.....................................72

Alone in the Jungle **Antonia Bolingbroke-Kent**...........88

Psiren Song **Beth French**.....................................100

Kayak-tivism **Carmen Kuntz**................................114

The Last of the Nomads **Cat Vinton**....................128

Soaking Up the Landscape **Emily Chappell**............142

Climb Every Mountain **Emma Svensson**................152

Ordinary Things with Extraordinary People
 Ewa Kalisiewicz..168

Tumping and Tripping **Hannah Maia**....................180

The Great Divide **Jenn Hill**..................................192

Pea and Gravel Soup **Julie Anne Christy**..............204

Truly Tough **Kate Rawles**.....................................214

Building Bridges **Misba Khan**...............................230

Moss / Tough Skin **Paula Flach**...........................240

My *Why* **Rea Kolbl**..254

In the Face of Fear **Rickie Cotter**.......................268

Learning to Be Tough **Sarah Outen**.....................278

It's Just Round the Corner **Vedangi Kulkarni**.......288

Acknowledgements..301

Copyright Acknowledgements.................................302

FOREWORD
JENNY TOUGH

Foreword   Jenny Tough

The length of time – milliseconds that go on for minutes – it takes until I hear the dead tree I've just pulled out of the mountainside splash into the river below is all I need to confirm the thought that was previously swirling, and now screaming, inside my head: one mistake, and I'm dead. The tree, now being carried through the impassible gorge by the raging white river, was meant to be my break on the climb. On an otherwise bare, precipitous, scree mountain flank, baking in the hot Kyrgyz summer sun, the small lone tree was the only feature I could rest on. And I really need a rest. Limbs shaking, sweat dripping, and the realization of my current consequences, I have no choice but to push onward and upward. No. Other. Choice.

It was my mistake. I know this. This isn't a mountain accident or an unfortunate turn of events. No, this was all me this time. I took a bad route. Chose a valley without thoroughly studying the contour lines. I followed a goat track – usually my only hope of decent footing – until I hit some landslides, which I delicately picked my way across. Up here in the Tien Shan, landslides are not out of place, and with the summer almost over, at least the avalanches have mostly settled. I'm not alarmed, and I continue on my course. But with an ominous rumble from above, the landslide I just picked my way over is awash with new boulders. I realize that I am not in a stable area. The boulders are not ankle-breakers; they're femur-breakers – not to mention the instant consequences should another landslide kick off while I'm in its path. There's no chance I'm going back that way, *no matter what happens.*

If I do break a femur, my hope of rescue out here, in the central Tien Shan, is quite limited. This country doesn't even have one single helicopter to send out. I know this, and I'm comfortable with the risk... Most of the time. But most of the time I don't make navigational errors like this one. Speeding away from the scary landslides, I turn the corner of the valley, and my heart drops all the way down to my shoes. The valley turns suddenly into a gorge. The slope I'm currently following goes all the way to 90 degrees, the thin goat track literally ending at a cliff edge. There is no way forward, and no way back.

I consider my options. There are really only two: go down into the river on my right, and swim through the gorge, or go up and over the mountain on my left, where I know it's a little gentler on the other side. I tiptoe down to the water's edge: it's deep, but moving fast, and not so deep that I wouldn't crack my skull on a protruding rock if I tried to float down it. I look up at the mountain: it's steep. Super-steep. I spend no more than a few minutes making my decision: death is slightly less likely on the mountain than the white water. I pull my GPS safety device out and put it around my neck, prepared if I need to drop my backpack at any point. I take a deep breath, and place my hands on the rock in front of me. *Don't look down.*

I have no idea, to this day, how long that climb took. It felt like 2 hours at least, but it's likely that it was less. I don't know how long it took, how high it was, or if there had been another option. I refuse to look at my gpx track for the day. I don't want to know. What I do know, is what my mind went through. They say your life flashes before your eyes, but it was my future that I saw instead. I realized all the things I wanted to do, clear visions of goals I wanted to accomplish, places I wanted to see, and more memories to be made with people I love. I focused on the placement of each foot and hand to ensure I had a chance of still getting to do them. I promised myself that if I survived this climb, I would call the expedition off. I would go home. They were right – I can't do this.

Three weeks earlier, I had landed in Bishkek, the capital of Kyrgyzstan, excited and ready to start my expedition: a solo and unsupported run across the central Tien Shan mountain range, which basically spanned the entire country. In all of my (considerable) research in preparing, I couldn't find any recording of anyone who had crossed this mountain range on foot, whether man or woman, walking or running. I had a chance at putting a world first to my name. It hadn't been the reason I decided to do it – it was already happening before I learned this – but my inner narcissist (who is usually fairly quiet) couldn't believe the luck.

The most intriguing bit of doing something that's never been done before is that there is no guidebook: you have to play Explorer and figure everything out yourself. You can't google anything. You have to find your way in the old-fashioned way, although I did rely heavily on satellite images of the mountains to design my route. I can't imagine how the explorers of old did without.

I spent more hours than I ever have on any project designing my expedition. I studied what few maps I could find, scoured the internet and any books that had ever touched Kyrgyzstan (I can tell you a lot about breeding the Kyrgyz horse, to give you an indication of how well scraped that barrel is), combed through any knowledge I could glean from anyone. There wasn't much. I made lists and went on training weekends in the Highlands and then made new lists. I was the definition of a good student. When I landed in Bishkek, I felt good. I knew I had done everything possible to make this work. Now all I had to do was buy some gas canisters for my stove (the only thing I didn't fly with), head to the eastern edge of the country, and run a thousand kilometres.

In the mountaineering office – which is really just a room with a few pieces of ancient Soviet alpinist equipment for rent – I found the gas canisters I needed. While fumbling for some *som* to pay with, the officer asked me what my "holiday plans" were in Kyrgyzstan.

"I'm going to run across Kyrgyzstan!" I told him with a confident grin. "I reckon it's about 1,000 kilometres, I've got a 12-kilogram pack with high-alpine camping equipment, and it should take me less than a month... err... Can't wait!"

He stared.

"... No," he slowly shook his head, "no. This can't be done. Kyrgyzstan is very big, and the mountains are very high. You'll see. This can't be done. No."

Unfortunately for him, my schedule for the day literally had nothing else but buying these canisters and spending some time adjusting to the altitude. I had time to wrangle. I took the bait.

"It can be done, I'll show you!" He followed my finger as I traced my route on the map, pointing out the valleys I would follow, the passes I would use, and the villages where I would resupply. Finally, a small nod of approval.

"OK, this is a good route actually... I think it can be done! But..." – and at this devastating moment, he paused to take a dramatic look up and down at me – "... not by you."

Ouch.

The following minutes of my life were at the height of mansplaining that I've had to endure as an outdoorswoman, and I'll never forget the glowing ember of rage as he made it clear that his assessment of my abilities was entirely based on nothing outside of my gender. I didn't bother to tell him how much mountain experience I already had. I didn't bother to tell him how well trained my legs were. I didn't even think to tell him how tough I can be. I did what we so often do: smiled sweetly, said something like, "OK, great, thanks", and left as fast as I could.

There's another intriguing bit about doing something that's never been done before, and the part that I wasn't aware of until that day, is that people generally believe it *can't* be done. They've never seen it, and probably for good reason. Every single day on that expedition (out of the days that I saw other humans) I was told it couldn't be done – sometimes with so much conviction that I was pointed back toward the nearest village, and even had the path blocked on a couple of more heated occasions.

———

My hands are sweating and blistering, and grabbing reliable holds is getting more and more difficult. I get stuck at one point, unsure where I can make my next move. I still haven't looked down – always look up. Look where you're going. And that better not be down. The long wait for the tree to hit the river below flashes in my mind again. That's how many seconds I'll be falling for if I miss this next move. With a grunt more akin to a battle cry, I push myself up the next ledge. I can see the top. I'm so close. *Just get there, and this whole expedition is finally over. Going home!* I scramble to the top, and on a curiously even, completely safe ground that gives way to a gentle, green, welcoming slope on the other side of the death-scree I've just climbed, I collapse into a heap. I cry harder than I can ever remember crying in my adult life. Adrenaline empties from my body in seconds and now I'm just a blubbering mess, letting the weight of everything that just went through my mind over the course of my climb really come out. I had to stay focused at the time, but the second it's over, out the emotions flood.

I didn't expect to cry like that, and while crying, I didn't expect the next thing I did either. After some time of full-on ugly-cry, I stopped, wiped my tears, fixed my ponytail, stood up, and continued as I had for the last twelve days. Just like that. I simply carried on running. I didn't fulfil my promise to quit, and it would be some time before I ever told anyone what had happened. I decided I should finish first.

————

After 23 days of navigating some of the most beautiful and formidable mountains in the world, I ran through the city gates of Osh in the south-west corner of the country. Even in the last 5 kilometres, as I finally let myself believe that I had been successful, cars were constantly pulling over to offer me a lift: insisting it was way too far to Osh, that I couldn't possibly run that far. My second and final big crying breakdown of the expedition occurred as I ran under those gates. I did it. Me. The unlikely candidate to become the first person to ever run all the way across Kyrgyzstan, all alone and unsupported. An impossible idea, and I proved it possible.

I never thought I was destined to be the sort of person who did those sorts of things. Neither did anyone else.

When I was a little girl, the kids at school used to laugh at me that my name was Tough. How ridiculous that a girl could be called Tough! I was embarrassed by it and wished that my family had been the Smiths or the Joneses or something. Little girls aren't Tough. Little girls are pretty and nice. That's what I learned at school. It was not right that I was called Tough. Point and laugh.

All grown up now, I wear my name with pride. What extreme good fortune that I should get to be called Tough! Every time my passport gets checked and the officer grins and asks, teasing, "So, are you really Tough?" I wink back. Hell yes I am. It's a great name. I love being Tough.

It isn't about being pretty and nice or not. That isn't part of the trait, and it isn't something binary where being tough diminishes any femininity. Tough means a lot of different things. It's not how many pull-ups you can do or who can win in a fight or how many chillis you can eat without crying. Your toughness is within. And your toughness is unique. It manifests itself in different ways. And it sure as anything does not identify with either gender more than the other.

I found my toughness for the first time in the mountains. Pursuing challenges that excited me but also scared me, and somehow getting through them, I showed myself that I actually deserved my name, that I was Tough. I still look at a looming mountain pass and shiver with a fear that I can't get up there. I've taken a few wrong turns over the years, like that valley in Kyrgyzstan, or looking up from my bivvy sac to see ten armed men in Morocco, or literally sprinting through illegal mines and coca fields in Bolivia, or limping on an infected wound in the desert... The list, unfortunately, really goes on. And I will continue to add to it – that's part of the path of life I've chosen, in truly challenging myself and the limits of my comfort zone. Any of those scenarios sound scary to me even now, but when the time came, I always rose to it, and later reflected that I had been so much tougher than I ever thought I was capable of. It grows my confidence and encourages me to keep expanding the limits of what I think I'm capable of, in all areas of my life – and I want that for everybody, especially women and girls.

Why Tough Women Adventure Stories?
For most of my life, I carried this fantasy that once I proved myself, no one would doubt me again. But, objectively speaking, I have proven myself by now. At the time of writing, I've completed four world-first solo expeditions like that one across Kyrgyzstan, won adventure races, been to six continents solo, and made a full-time career in the outdoors. If I could meet with my fifteen-year-old self, she would be delighted, and she would assume that no one doubts me any more. But they do – if they only have my appearance to judge me on, that is.

Perhaps that is one thing that I love so dearly about spending time in the wilderness – it's the greatest equalizer. The mountains don't care what gender you identify with, how old you are, who you love, how you speak. They don't give a toss. You are free out there. But on so many occasions in my life, I've been warned against going to this sanctuary – because I'm a woman. It never used to bother me, to be honest. I always believed in my own abilities and knew the strength of my years of experience, so I just ignored the comments and carried on anyway. But, what about the women and girls who don't have that? What about someone new to the outdoor world? Are we really sending a message that this is not an arena for women to venture into?

The following pages are stories from some of the most badass outdoorswomen out there. They are stories of grit, love, determination, passion and trailblazing. All of these authors have discovered their unique inner toughness and used it to follow a path in life of their own choosing. My hope with this book is that it will show the many faces of toughness, and encourage everyone – men and women, boys and girls – to reassess our culture's perceptions about who does or doesn't belong in the outdoors (hint: everyone; no one). I also wanted to give a voice to some incredible role models who have great stories to tell. The truth is, the outdoor industry is actually full of women, but when it comes to the highest level of media, such as what we see on television, the demographic dwindles to one, and so the wider community believes that tough outdoorspeople fit one single mould.

But change is happening, and by giving a platform to the voices who are igniting that change – a platform like a book, for example – we continue to grow. I've always believed in the power of storytelling – stories that leave an impact, stories that people will remember. The following pages are filled with storytellers I admire. The authors in this book will take you around the world, with challenges ranging from races and world records, to battles with their own bodies and minds, to independent pursuits and personal growth. The stories in this book, and the women who wrote them, all embody what it means to be tough.

WILD AT HEART

ALIÉNOR LE GOUVELLO

Aliénor le Gouvello fostered a passion for travelling and embarking on adventures around the globe from a young age. A woman of French nationality and Australian residency, she has completed a 900-kilometre horseback trek in Mongolia, a sidecar motorbike expedition from Siberia to Paris, a 580-kilometre endurance horse race in Mongolia in which she finished first and a motorbike trip in India.

In Australia, she has travelled extensively through remote Australia in her position working with indigenous youth, which is where she fell in love with the outback's wide-open spaces. In 2015, she set out on her longest solo adventure so far: a 5,330-kilometre trek along the National Trail in Australia on horseback with the aim of dedicating her ride to the plight of the brumby (the Australian wild horse). Australia has the largest population of wild horses in the world but they are viewed as pests because they are not native to Australia. To manage their population the government has used very cruel methods, including aerial culling. Aliénor wants to promote more humane methods of rehoming them.

She recently published a novel of her expedition on the National Trail titled *Sur la Piste Sauvage* with French publisher Arthaud. As she describes it herself, "life is one big adventure".

Find out more about Aliénor at:
F: Wild at Heart Australia
I: Wild_at_Heart_Australia

But the true voyagers are only those who leave
Just to be leaving; hearts light, like balloons,
They never turn aside from their fatality
And without knowing why they always say: "Let's go!"

From "The Voyage" by Charles Baudelaire

Perhaps it all began the day I participated in a bush race in the Australian desert. I was invited to enter a horse race – me, the only woman and with white skin. Lost in the desert, in a furnace-like, dusty atmosphere, against all odds, I won the race in front of an audience of males who were stunned that a woman could beat them.

Or perhaps it all started when I met my ex-partner, who introduced me to this country. It is thanks to him that I fell in love with the outback and decided to work with indigenous youth. These children seem neglected by the world, yet are still so enthusiastic and brimming with life. I tried for over ten years to give them the best of me, my energy, my imagination. I learned their language, traditions and way of life, especially their unique way of understanding nature and merging with the universe. Living in remote communities taught me to make do with little, to be self-sufficient and always find a solution.

I have come to love this red dirt that I walk on with my bare feet. I am not scared of this nature – it never betrays me, even in the toughest situations. It is also thanks to this experience that I came across my first brumbies, these majestic wild horses, so resilient and tough but considered a pest by most. The desert is full of them. It was also in one of the indigenous communities that I adopted my dog, Foxy, a dingo cross (a cross with the Australian wild dog), my most precious friend.

Shortly after I decided to trek the National Trail solo with three brumbies, Cooper, River and Roxanne, a journey of 5,330 kilometres across this raw continent from south to north, I stumbled by coincidence on the story of a woman, Robyn Davidson. She had walked across Australia from east to west with camels. If she could survive the trek across the deserts, I thought I should be able to manage my expedition along the spine of the east coast of Australia.

After a year and a half of preparation, training wild horses, researching the trail, acquiring the right equipment and organizing the logistics, I set off. I spent 13 months trekking in all conditions imaginable – rough terrain, diverse weather and countless obstacles. One packhorse for all my camping and horse equipment and food rations, one riding horse and a horse at rest, rotating them every day. We became a family, my horses, my dog, Fox, and I. We created an intimate bond, travelling and living together. We shared camp life; they never trampled on anything. I came to know all of their intricate and different characters. At first it was very hard to find our pace, three horses travelling in harmony led by me, but after a few months and as the terrain eased we got better.

I had to take a break to bypass a cyclone, endured a trip to a hospital in Townsville, experienced hunger from rationing supplies and the exhaustion and pain from the tropical fever which had started attacking my joints – I was diagnosed with Ross River fever but disregarded the doctor's advice to quit for a while. Just a week from finishing, my next challenge began: a throbbing, lightning-sharp pain in my heel, which instilled in me the fear of not being able to carry on.

Cat, my amazing photographer friend, had joined me on foot for the last few weeks. I actually knew her for 5 minutes when I met her in London over a year ago through a common acquaintance. I had told her about my project and she volunteered to join me to document some of my expedition. It was a life gift to have met her and she followed through and came. She is the most resilient woman I know and a very talented photographer. Passionate about nomadic culture, she has had the experience of living with some of the last migratory tribes of the world. Her extraordinary ability to blend into people's lives and document their habits and culture is truly inspiring. During our time together on the trail, I walked on foot about a third of the day, but she walked all day every day with a backpack, enduring the heat, steep terrain and thick vegetation. We formed a really special friendship. She couldn't have arrived at a better time.

———

The fever makes me lethargic and weak but also gives me the most excruciating pain in my joints. In order just to function I take ridiculous amounts of painkillers and anti-inflammatory medication. I can hardly move my fingers, wrists and ankles. I resort to riding all day and falling off my horse in the late afternoon, screaming in pain as I try to stand with the immense pressure on my ankles. Cat's enthusiasm, help and easy-going attitude are a godsend. It's 15 June and I think, but with no certitude, that today marks the day we clock over 5,000 kilometres. I'm not attached to the number but the destination. Cooktown is my focus: it is the milestone in itself.

That night we set up camp by a lake. Under a starry sky, next to the shimmering light of my campfire and with Fox's head on my lap, I anticipate my arrival in Cooktown. What will I do next? Three years of my life are coming to an end. I haven't thought beyond this point and the prospect of having a "normal life" is pretty daunting. In the morning, we are charmed by a beautiful sunrise reflecting in the lake, little clouds like a field of cotton against a soft light blue. Fifteen days from arriving in the town that has achieved mythical status in my imagination, I pull out my last guidebook of the National Trail. I am doing the trail backward, so I'm nearly at the start. After the ritual of 2 hours to pack down camp and get the horses ready, Cat and I are on the move again. The landscape is magic as we move along a ridge overlooking other mountains. This early in the morning the light is piercing through fog and shining on the bright, huge, white eucalyptus trunks and their umbrella of blue-green leaves. Scattered around like the indigenous elders of this country are a few "blackboys", or grass trees, which have this fascinating silhouette of a lean, black, charcoal-like trunk with a big, green, Afro-style hairdo. This native plant can grow to be hundreds of years old and, in some cases, up to 600 years old.

We are coming down a mountain toward civilization, where I've organized a farrier to meet us and attend to my horses' feet. After 3,000 kilometres with the horses unshod or wearing "hoof boots" which can break easily, get lost and are extremely hard to put on, I decided to shoe them because they are foot-sore. If I had begun this journey with my horses shod, I would have had to include special stops for shoeing every six or so weeks. This is very costly and logistically not an easy task when you're in the middle of nowhere most of the time (the first three months were the most remote part of the trail).

We negotiate the descent of the Great Dividing Range toward a small country town called Mutchilba, traversing old tobacco, fruit and rice plantations. Throughout the day I manage to forget the pain I am enduring by focusing on our navigation and surroundings. Every now and then I let out an uncontrollable scream of pain when I execute an unsuitable movement.

Once at Mutchilba we wait for the farrier, grazing the horses on the roadside. After a short while, a Toyota four-wheel drive towing a trailer pulls up beside us. A gigantic long-bearded, red-haired brute with a cap and weird yellow glasses comes out to greet us. He is friendly enough, like most Australians, so all is good. He gets on with his job of caring for my horses' feet as a client of his pulls up to say hi. She seems intrigued by our journey and invites us to camp on her property nearby. The campsite mentioned in the guidebook didn't seem too appealing so we accept the kind offer.

Cat jumps in with the farrier, along with our gear, and I take the opportunity to ride my horse bareback for a bit of a change. I am so happy to be able to trot and canter for once, bareback and leading a horse on either side of me. Cooper, River and Roxanne think it's fun too, to be free of the dead weight of the pack saddle that keeps us at a walk on the trail. When we arrive at the property I notice a smirk on Cat's face. She is the smiliest person I know, but this particular smile has a story. I find out later that the farrier's first question when she hopped into the car was: "So yous two are a bunch of carpet munchers?" with his real Queenslander accent. Cat got confused and responded that she had been eating fine on the trail but soon realized what he meant – his insinuation that two women travelling together in the bush had to be gay! I can't stop laughing. Carpet munchers – what a poet.

Three days after leaving Mutchilba we climb the Great Dividing Range again in the most insane zigzags. It's quite common to be heading south at times before heading north again – the most frustrating feeling when you are so close to your goal and have been on the trail for over a year. We are heading toward Mount Molloy, winding through rugged and isolated old mining ranges, up and down a hundred gullies and bushy hills as far as the eye can see. It's becoming harder and harder to find our path as the "track" is increasingly overgrown. At a fork with several faint tracks, I hesitate and take a break to contemplate my navigation. Nothing makes sense. Reading the trail guidebooks backward has proven to be extremely challenging, especially when they read: "head west after the gully heading toward the next ridge, follow the top of the ridge heading north until a bunya pine, then follow the old fence…" but there's no fence any more!

I waste time trying to make sense of these mud maps, or hand-drawn maps, and notes that are over 30 years old. Time is precious when you have to travel 30–40 kilometres a day at a walk, find water, find your next campsite, take care of your horses and make camp before dark. Frustrated and running out of sunlight, I decide to follow my nose and use my compass to head up a faint track in the direction we are supposed to be going. Cat trusts me so far – we never get lost.

After a couple of hours of going up and down steep gullies, Cat and my horses are sweating profusely but don't complain. I can't walk because of the pain but after 3 hours and looking back at Cat's bright red face I get off and insist she takes my place on the horse. We are both as stubborn as each other. Luckily, I'm riding Roxanne today, my rock. I put Cat's backpack on and walk up a ridge, where I hope to see something and make sense of where we are. My nose hasn't been so good in this situation. The track I chose has taken us in the wrong direction for the last hour, but I had hoped it would change to a more favourable course. At the top of the ridge as we catch our breath, I look all around me and see nothing – nothing that looks like the old mining town we want to reach. Eventually I notice a tiny bit of smoke. Miles and miles away. That has to be it. There is no way we will get there in daylight. We need to find water before dark and backtrack tomorrow. I tell Cat we are not lost – we are just off track a little...

I remember going across a gully a few kilometres back with a couple of puddles of water. Maybe I can find more water. When we arrive, I leave Cat and the horses and start up the rocky gully on foot. The Aborigines taught me that where there are big bulging rocks, there could be water... bingo! A nice waterhole with clear enough water for us and the horses – so lucky. Unfortunately, there is not much grass for the horses, but I fed them well at Mutchilba; they will cope. I am so relieved. We build camp in a hurry as the sun disappears behind the ranges. Tomorrow we will leave extra early and backtrack with the hope of finding our way to Kingsborough, a lost gold mine which counts one habitant, a gold prospector who arrived 30 years ago and remains part of the ruins.

A couple of days on, we are still on our way to Mount Molloy, a historic mining site whose population has declined to 273 inhabitants. Mines are running out; young people are going to the cities. Mount Molloy has one main street, a few houses on either side and electric poles. In the past, a strong Chinese community cultivated vegetable gardens to feed miners.

An update indicates that the trail to get to Mount Molloy is closed for the next three days. The trail is a living route and access changes according to the weather conditions and the owners of the large ranches. The route covered by maps nine to twelve in the guide is closed because of the lack of water and access to the route. More bushwhacking it is. As nerve-racking as it can be, it is also the most exhilarating and rewarding way to travel. When I find my way through the bush reading mud maps and relating them to the country it is very satisfying. East is our destination, across the divide again, toward the ocean. It's been long awaited! I've been longing to camp with my crew on the beach and this section of the trail is the only one close enough to the coast to allow it.

Following a mostly dry riverbed, the area covered by map nine turns out to be OK in regard to navigation, but the only water available is less than appealing. A stagnant puddle of water and no grass is the only option for my companions. It's been a few days of very dry country and very little pasture for my dear friends. Rid of their loads, cleaned of their sweat, caressed and thanked, my steeds park themselves in front of us to beg as we have our little snack of sardines and biscuits. I explain to them that we've run out of treats and that I'll make it up to them in Mount Molloy. I am ashamed as I eat in front of them – it breaks my heart when I can't provide for them.

The next morning, it's foggy, wet and hard to see the landscape around us. When bushwhacking I often follow cattle or wild-horse pads. ("Pads" is an Australian term for the tracks animals make through the bush to get from their grazing place to water or other grazing spots.) That way, if the terrain is challenging, like going through gullies or rivers, you know other animals have made it through. It's tough going in wet, thick, scrubby country and Cat, who's not very tall, loses our track from time to time and calls out to locate us. I stop regularly to study the landscape and choose our way, navigating through the bush. My horses travel in single file. We are all soaked. The gear gets heavier when it's wet, and my Driza-Bone feels like it weighs a tonne.

After 6 hours of walking uninterrupted, I land exactly where I'd hoped! Back on an old stone path built long ago by pioneers. I can just see the remains of the path through the overgrown vegetation. We have been following this old route for a while when my horses come to a standstill with their ears pricked up in alert. Galloping out of the bushes ahead of us comes a mob of bay wild horses. Cat just misses them – she is too far back. It is such a beautiful experience to witness these animals in their environment, and I feel so grateful.

We are almost out of the Hann Tableland National Park and this difficult section. What an epic few days. We've managed to get through despite the giant spear grass and the fact that this section of the trail is so isolated from mankind that nature has claimed it back. After a little break in Mount Molloy to fill my companions' bellies and pick up our food rations, we are a day away from the coast. The landscape has changed radically, from dry, hard and rocky into luxuriant tropical forests. We descend to the coast using an old coach road called the Bump

Track. In the early days of colonization, it was a vital link for miners and settlers between Port Douglas and the hinterland after the discovery of gold in the area in 1877. All the artillery and explosives needed for the tin, copper and gold mines were transported by wagons pulled by horses and bullocks. A four-tonne wagon would have required 36 horses to pull it. Many of the livestock perished on this trek.

The path sinks into a dense tropical jungle made up of gigantic trees. I feel miniature in this thick forest dotted with rays of light. Eventually a clearing through the trees offers a magnificent view of the ocean in the distance. This vision is overwhelmingly gratifying; up until this point the trail has sat 50–100 kilometres from the coast, so it's the first time I have seen the ocean since I left 13 months ago. Once we make it down the range, sugar cane, palm trees and civilization replace the bush.

We are in a small town called Mossman, a week from Cooktown. After being stranded for four days under buckets of rain and camping in the stables of a rodeo ground, Cat helps me find a camping spot on the beach. Although locals have warned us about a 6-metre saltwater crocodile, I am determined to stay.

Sadly, the next day Cat leaves us as she has other commitments and a plane to catch. We have trekked hard for six weeks with very little rest with the aim to reach the end together and the fever has really broken me. I need to recharge my batteries and there's nothing like the ocean for that. The scenery is magical and I jump on Cooper bareback for a gallop on the beach.

Although the location is a fairy tale, I have pushed too far and my immune system is letting me down. I have this pain in my heel that hasn't gone away for a few days and is now throbbing terribly. The heat, redness and the abscess swelling suggest to me that it could be a staph infection. I know what it is because I have had it before, when living in remote Aboriginal communities, and they don't just go away. I have been ignoring it and it has got to the point where the throbbing pain keeps me up all night screaming. So close and yet still not there – I can't believe it. By the time I manage to get my horses to safety and seek help to get to hospital, the doctors tell me the infection is almost in the bone and could have been fatal.

After a heavy dose of intravenous antibiotics, getting cut open and being forced to rest for four days, I disregard the doctors' advice of bed rest and leave to get back on my horses. My foot is strapped in a plastic bag and I'm unable to walk without a lot of pain, but I push on, trusting my horses through another tough section of the trail. The CREB Track, renowned for being a very challenging four-wheel-drive track, is closed due to rain. Being clay and extremely steep, the conditions are too dangerous for vehicles, but I have managed to get permission from the council to pass through on horseback. At my absolute wits' end, with two open wounds (on my heel and on my leg) in wet weather, I forge ahead. I have to cross a deep and wide river infested with crocodiles with my foot in a plastic bag and navigate the CREB Track in slippery conditions. I am joined by a film crew who want to capture the end of my odyssey. I hate them being there and it really slows me down. I am so determined to finish. So close. I am in a world of pain and I know ignoring the doctors' advice was not the safe option, but I have the end in sight.

On 20 July I arrive in Cooktown. I get off my horse struggling to hold back a couple of tears, limping and staggering with my foot still in a plastic bag. I thank my horses, the heroes in this story who have carried me all this way. It is so surreal

I don't know what words could best describe my emotions. A combination of happy, sad, utterly exhausted, lost, confused, proud and so relieved it is over. Three years of my life have come to an end.

It's only now, with some perspective, that I truly see and appreciate the growth, the experiences and the challenges the National Trail gave me. I used to say anyone could do this with the right preparation and yes, it was key for me to complete the entire trail with horses in such good condition, but it's a lot more than that. Anyone can prepare, but not everyone will actually go and finish a 13-month trek with all of the trials and tribulations that it presents. It took sheer determination and commitment. I fantasized that I had it before I left and, on reflection, I now know that I've honed it to a level I could never have expected.

This wonderful experience cultivated within me an even deeper respect and connection with nature, animals and the planet we live on. The desire to thrive and nurture that in my everyday life has become paramount. The experience was enriching and fulfilling, providing countless challenges that have strengthened my character and emphasized my ability to push the boundaries. Some days I wanted to curl up under a tree and wait for someone to come and get me, but each and every time I restored my body just enough to keep going. Our comfort zone is all in the mind. Our bodies have the ability to excel way beyond the limits we initially set for ourselves.

MODERN-DAY EXPLORER

ANN DANIELS

Ann Daniels is a mother of four children, a polar explorer and international speaker.

She began her unlikely career in the polar regions shortly after leaving her bank job when she had triplets. She saw an advert and in a moment of madness applied and was selected from over 200 women to take part in her first North Pole expedition, a relay to the North Pole. From these humble beginnings, she went on to conquer the South Pole, after which she returned to the Arctic, sledge-hauling from Nunavut to the geographic North Pole, and became the first woman in history to ski to both poles in an all-women team.

Having fallen in love with the polar regions, Ann has spent the past ten years helping scientists understand the fragile ends of our planet. She has sledge-hauled over 2,000 miles, completed over ten polar expeditions and endured temperatures as low as –50°C while dealing with polar bear encounters. Her most recent expeditions saw Ann working with NASA and the European Space Agency.

Her achievements have been recognized by *The Guinness Book of Records*, the Pride of Britain Awards and the Foreign Office. Ann has appeared on TV and radio and is passionate about climate change and the world we live in.

Find out more about Ann at:
W: www.anndaniels.com
T/I: @AnnDanielsGB

As we lay in our frozen sleeping bags at the end of the world, we were suddenly roused out of our cold fitful sleep in the early hours by the loud sound of ice grinding toward us. It was dark outside and we lay for a while praying that the breaking and churning noise didn't indicate the breaking up of the solid pan where, after an exhausting day hauling our sledges across the ice on the Arctic Ocean, we'd pitched our tent. I could feel the butterflies in my stomach as I realized the threat was very real and our lives could be in danger. I wasn't completely sure if I was afraid for our safety or if it was simply the dread of having to get out of my vaguely warm sleeping bag to check on the ice and potentially move camp. We listened carefully and, eventually, as the noise got louder and louder and closer and closer, we knew we'd have to get out and assess our situation.

———

I was in a three-man Hilleberg tent in the middle of the Arctic Ocean with Pen Hadow and Martin Hartley. Pen Hadow is the first man to have walked solo and unsupported from Canada to the North Pole and has completed many Arctic and Antarctic expeditions. He is highly regarded in the polar community and it was he who put together the women's team for my first expedition on the ice in 1997. It is because of this man that, at the age of 33, I discovered my love of expedition life in the polar regions. Martin Hartley is an amazing expedition and adventure photographer who has spent over 400 days working in the polar regions and is also well known for capturing spectacular imagery in deserts, mountains and many other environments.

It was the first time I had been on the ice with both men, but we quickly formed a tight-knit bond. It was 2009, early spring, when the days are short, the temperatures cold and the nights are still dark. I had been asked to join the team as the pathfinder, camp cook and to manage the day-to-day logistics of a scientific expedition whose aims were to measure the thickness of the sea ice and collect data on the surface features along a large transect of the Arctic Ocean. We were working with scientists around the world, including NASA, so it was a big deal – or at least it was as far as I was concerned.

The expedition was planned to take around 73 days and I had been asked to physically lead the ice team by Pen Hadow, the true leader of this important scientific venture, whose brainchild it was. It was essential that he concentrated on collecting the data and relaying it to the ice experts and scientists working on understanding this vital part of our planet. He therefore needed someone he could trust to find a route through the jumble of ice and keep the expedition on track. Martin was the expedition photographer. As well as completing our research, we also wanted to share our findings with the world in general and hopefully make some small difference to people's perception of this part of the world – and what better way to do it than with emotive photographs.

The Arctic is warming at twice the rate of the rest of the planet and the ice covering the Arctic Ocean is disappearing fast, with disastrous consequences for the wildlife and indigenous people who call it home. Since my first expedition in 1997, I had seen first-hand the difference in the icescape: less ice that had been around for more than one year, growing thicker each winter; more thin ice, open water and much more movement in the ice as it has more room to shift and crack. I was therefore delighted when Pen asked me to join this important expedition. The Arctic had given me the opportunity for a new and exciting career at the ends of the world, and I had fallen in love with its beauty and splendour. During my time up there, I had developed a passion for this austere wilderness and I cared about what I could see happening to the place I loved so much. To be able to do something, no matter how small, to help experts understand the changes occurring was both a privilege and an honour.

In early February 2009, I left my partner Tom and four children, Sarah, Rachel, Lucy and Joseph, and flew up to Resolute Bay in Nunavut to make the final preparations for the expedition. We needed to check all our equipment, make sure we knew the protocols for taking accurate scientific measurements and pack everything into our sledges. I also needed some time to shift from normal life to that of an explorer. I felt a weight of responsibility on my shoulders for the team. I knew I would be at the front of this team as long as the expedition lasted, making decisions about the route and the safety of the different types of ice we would need to cross for many miles, and I didn't want to let anyone down.

On 28 February, we were finally dropped off by a Twin Otter plane in the middle of the Arctic Ocean at 81° 41' North. As it circled and left us behind, I felt both scared and excited. The beginning of any expedition is the hardest as you face the unknown ahead, but the possibilities are also endless and there is a feeling of mild euphoria along with the butterflies.

We had been up since 2 a.m. and it was late in the day when we landed so we made the decision to ski for a couple of hours and then stop for the evening. The sledges felt heavy and it was slow-going but there were no major obstacles and after 2 hours we were pleased to have completed 2 nautical miles on our first day.

On the second day the temperature dropped slightly and visibility was low. When this happens it often means there's going to be movement and change in the ice. The ice on the Arctic Ocean moves constantly. The terrain we travelled on was mainly made up of pans of ice, open water, thin ice and pressure ridges (which can be metres in height). After a couple of hours of fairly flat solid ice, we came across our first major tear in the icy surface. It resembled a large river and had partly frozen. I tested the ice with my ski pole, jabbing at it with all my strength, and went across to the other side first to check it was safe. Pen came next and, as his heavy sledge full of scientific equipment hit the ice, I could hear it crack slightly. He got to the other side safely and Martin came across last of all, making sure not to follow either my or Pen's tracks across the thin ice. Our first crossing was complete and we all felt relieved that our ice skills were still strong.

During the day we crossed a few other tricky areas of thin ice, skirted several small areas of open water and hauled our sledges over some high ridges, but all in all the day was fairly uneventful. We put the tent up, did our nightly drilling duties, ate supper and went to bed happy with our progress.

That was the evening of the ice movement.

We were shaken out of our calm confidence with the terrible reminder that out here it's the Arctic that is ultimately in control, not us. As we lay there in the cold dark tent, listening to the grumbling and rumbling outside, the stark reality of our mission began to hit home. We would be out here for days on end, living in extreme temperatures, on a fragile crust of ice, with no other humans for thousands of miles. The Twin Otter plane is used to support expeditions in this area as it is small enough and robust enough to land on small patches of ice. They are stationed at Resolute Bay, which is two days' flight away for such a small plane. There could be no quick rescue when danger reared its ugly head. We were alone and reliant on each other, whatever came our way. Thankfully, I had the best team with me. I was hugely relieved and thankful when Pen volunteered to go and check what was happening outside and immensely grateful I hadn't chosen life as a photographer, as Martin, of course, also had to go out and capture the experience for posterity and for everyone following our progress in the land of civilization.

They couldn't have been gone more than 15 minutes, but listening to the growing noise on my own in the dark was unnerving and I was glad when they eventually returned – although the news wasn't good. The currents and power of nature were eating the ice and breaking it up constantly, crushing it and fracturing it closer and closer to the tent. It was unsafe to stay where we were as the solid base around us would soon be a mass of broken ice, snow and water. We had to move. Getting out of the tent in the middle of the night when the temperature is below –30°C and everything is moving under your feet is a unique and terrifying experience. Keeping a cool head is most important of all and we worked together quickly as a team to pack everything up and move on to the next pan of ice which appeared safe and solid. At least for the time being. It can't have taken longer than an hour to move but getting warm again once we had set up our new camp took forever.

Far too soon morning arrived, and I began my daily routine of melting the ice on the zip of my sleeping bag before clambering out in the freezing cold to brush the icy rime from the tent walls. I then lit our small metal cookers, melting snow and preparing breakfast before the long day's skiing began. On days like this it was the thought of why we were out here in the first place that kept me going and convinced me that our efforts were for "the Arctic Ocean", which made it bearable.

While I prepared our meal, Pen was checking our electronic equipment. He returned with the terrible news that the surface radar we were pulling that was supposed to measure the ice as we skied along wasn't working at all. We were devastated. We were drilling the ice each night, as agreed by various scientific bodies and writing down with a simple pencil on a card every surface feature of the ice, but the radar was a huge part of the expedition. We had tested it on several occasions in the High Arctic the year before and it worked every time, but up here, when it mattered most, it completely failed us.

We spent the day in the tent trying to fix the problem. Things had changed in the past ten years and we had satellite telephones, so we were able to speak to the guys who designed and built our bespoke radar. After a whole day of trying everything, we had to admit defeat. We tried to mend it again and again throughout the expedition with no success. It was a huge blow to Pen in particular after all his hard work.

We had to console ourselves with the fact that we could still drill through the ice each night and take accurate measurements of the ice, snow and freeboard (the distance between the water that rose through the hole we had drilled and the top of the ice), we could still take snow depth measurements throughout the day and of course make notes of the surface features. All of which were vital to understanding the changes on the Arctic Ocean.

As teammates we were very close and helped each other whenever possible, but the make-up of our roles meant that for long periods of time we were alone with our duties. I spent all day up front finding a route, only connecting with Pen and Martin every 75 minutes for a 10-minute break to eat and drink and then set out again alone up front. At the end of the day I entered the tent to cook dinner, while Martin and Pen struggled in the cold outside to drill through the thick ice. When they had finished their duties they entered the main part of the tent while I cooked in the vestibule. While I could hear them talk and they were careful to include me in their conversations, it was often difficult to hear with the roaring cookers and at times it felt lonely. Cold and lonely. The temperature was so low in that part of the tent, by the time the steam hit the roof of the tent it froze. I could barely feel my fingers and toes, which were stiff and wooden as I worked. When the last drink was made I turned one cooker off and joined the men, bringing the second cooker with me. We drank our final drink together, drawing some warmth from the cooker. It was the best part of every day. A moment of shared companionship before turning the cooker off and allowing the ever-present cold to creep its way back into the tent.

The temperature dropped to −40°C on the thermometer the next day and we began to suffer frozen fingers and toes throughout the day. For the next seven days, the temperature was between –37°C and –40°C, with winds of up to 25 kilometres per hour. Adding wind chill took us down to –56°C. It was true hell. We were living in extreme conditions and we all suffered from cold injuries. Martin got bad frostbite on his big toe, which blistered, went purple and looked like a small aubergine. His pain was excruciating and I constantly looked back to make sure the pace was manageable for all of us. I had sore fingers and toes, but when I saw Martin my own suffering paled into insignificance.

In severe cold the sledges stuck to the ice, making travel slow and difficult. The terrain started off with the usual flat pans with ridges and broken ice, but we spent very long hours in huge rubble fields where the ice was so broken it took all three of us to get one sledge through every inch of the mess, which we then had to repeat with the other sledges.

I was almost relieved when I woke up on day 11 and on checking the weather discovered there was a storm raging outside. It was impossible to travel and we had to stay in the tent. It gave us time to recover, although of course not enough time to heal Martin's toe. Not only had we deteriorated physically but so had our equipment. All our jackets had a broken zip down one side and we each sewed them closed, practically sewing ourselves into our jackets. We could undo them at night with the zip on the other side but couldn't manage it during the day if we needed to loosen the jacket when going to the toilet. It was better and warmer to sew them than use safety pins, which left gaps for the cold to get in.

Having a storm day is a double-edged sword. Living life on the edge of existence is debilitating and being able to rest was a relief, but we were all aware of the importance of the work we were undertaking and guilt took a seat in our minds.

Thankfully, the storm lasted just one day. The temperature was still −40°C the following day but, with only a light breeze to contend with, we were confident of making good progress. The light was beautiful and calm as we exited the tent and our surroundings looked like a scene in a cemetery, with small, upended slabs of ice bathed in a weak mist. It felt soothing rather than eerie.

Life in the Arctic is full of extremes and we crossed many areas of cracked ice, huge ridges and large obstacles. While the cold was painful, it did mean that any open water exposed by splitting ice quickly froze and we often skied along newly frozen ice that was solid and flat. A sledger's dream. We crossed polar bear tracks on a couple of occasions, reminding us of the need to stay vigilant at all times.

On day 19 we were due a resupply. As the purpose of the expedition was scientific research we had regular resupplies so we could send out data and images and replace used or damaged equipment such as sharp drill blades. Cutting through metres of ice quickly blunted the ends, which needed replacing regularly. The Twin Otter, which is used for resupply, needs a clear runway on the ice to land. On previous expeditions it could take days of scouting on the ground to find a pan big enough for a landing. With NASA as our partners, we had the privilege of being able to receive satellite images to identify possible runways, and during our daily calls to base camp in which we let them know our situation along the way they gave us clear coordinates of where to find thick flat ice. It was a game changer and took the anxiety out of searching for a suitable landing. Clean clothes and extra treats arrived with the flight and increased morale hugely. Martin had extra hand warmers and socks brought in for his feet. We felt a certain sense of renewed hope for the journey ahead.

Our mantra became "Our sledges can only get lighter, the temperature can only get warmer" (as each day brought us closer to the Arctic summer). We felt as if the impossible had now become possible. The temperature increased slightly after the resupply day. It was still −30°C but −30°C is much more manageable than −40°C. It feels less frightening and more about physical hardship rather than survival or constantly fighting the onset of frostbite. Even our frozen rations seemed more palatable and easier to eat. Chunks of chocolate melted quicker, nuts didn't feel like concrete to eat and flapjack almost had a taste.

During the next five days, the ridges were constant and we were exhausted at the end of each day from pulling heavy sledges, but we didn't hit too much in the way of obstacles to stop our progress. Beautiful circles of light known as "sun dogs" circled the weak sun and slowly we progressed across the ice. Our routines were familiar and the days were a mixture of distance gained, data captured and photographs taken.

A third of the way through our twenty-fourth day, however, we came across a split in the ice 100 metres across which had frozen most of the way to the other side but there was a 2-metre gap of open water on the opposite side barring our way. We stayed on the southern side of the split where the ice was stronger and as I constantly skied back and forth across the stretch of thin ice to check the opposite side, I came across open water each time and had to return to the team and try again further along. It took over three hours to find a crossing point. Three hours in which we could only go west rather than our intended northerly direction. No sooner had we crossed this than another river of open water stopped us in our tracks, taking hours to cross. These splits are known to expeditions as "leads" and we didn't want to stop until we had cleared the lead and reached better ice. The sun now shone for 24 hours a day and we skied until 10.30 p.m., until finally we reached a flat area of ice where we could stop for the night and look forward to better progress the next day.

Remarkably, on day 25 we woke to temperatures of –25°C, but with the warm weather came light snowfall and poor visibility. There was no sun, complete cloud cover, no contrast and no definition. Navigating north required all my skills. I don't use a GPS to navigate in the polar regions. In these temperatures the screens don't work properly and it would take more batteries than I can pull to keep them going. I occasionally use a compass in bad weather, but it also doesn't work well so close to the magnetic pole, so I navigate with the sun when it's visible. When it's not, I try and fix a direction with the slow compass at the start of the skiing session and then, using immense amounts of concentration, I squint at the faint lines of the snow, watch the angle of small snow specks blowing across my bright red skis, keep my skis equidistantly apart and make sure my daughter's ribbon (which I have attached to the top of my ski pole) blows in the same angle. Anything to keep us going direct north. It was exhausting, but thankfully by the end of the day the sun came out and navigation came easily once more.

During the next 15 days before our second resupply, the temperature fluctuated between –30°C and –40°C, with variable ice conditions. Sometimes it was huge ridges and the going was slow. Occasionally we had open water to negotiate, but mostly it was small pans of ice covered in snow and ending in moderately sized ridges. As a team we worked to our strengths. It was cold and back-breaking but we each had our own role to play. The men, with their greater strength, pulled heavier sledges and did more of the outside work in the evening, but I was always up first at 5.30 a.m. to light the cookers and get the breakfast ready and last in my sleeping bag at night. Everyone gave everything they had.

The second resupply came on day 40 and during those 40 days we had gone through hell. I had sobbed quietly when exhaustion came calling during the long sledging days or when my feet and hands suffered from the pain of the cold in the hostile, dark kitchen. It was the comradeship we shared that got me through. People often ask me how I keep going when it's truly awful and I never really know how to answer except to say that there is no other option. I can't simply give up and let my colleagues down. There is no plan B, so keep going we must. During the first half of the expedition, which was the hardest part by a million miles, we survived and endured unimaginable hardships together. We were all pared back to our true selves. There was no hiding in those conditions, and through the bad and the good, we came through it together. I'm not saying there weren't disagreements, but there were only a few and it was never over anything serious. We had each other's back at all times and that made the pain and discomfort bearable. We had some magical moments when we came across fox tracks and saw a seal, but seeing wildlife in those early dark and cold days was rare. We had each other and that was it.

As well as replacing our scientific equipment, the resupply gave us food, fuel, a change of clothes, letters and treats from our family and the team back in the UK and a new sleeping bag each, which was heavenly. Our sleeping bags had frozen to varying degrees and were horrid to climb into at night. For the first time in the expedition I slept solidly and didn't wake up throughout the night shivering from the cold.

The expedition was definitely a game of two halves. Shortly after the second resupply, the temperature dropped to –26°C. Our sledges were heavy again and we battled through the broken ice which littered the Arctic Ocean, but the change in temperature made a huge difference to our morale and progress. It wasn't warm by any stretch of the imagination, but we weren't in constant pain from the cold and could think and act much more quickly and clearly.

With the warmer weather came more ice movement and open water. We came across large areas of rough ice boulders trapped between thin ice. They looked like hundreds of frozen cauliflowers stuck together. They were difficult to ski over, but for the most part it was possible to find a path slowly and carefully. One area, however, suddenly began to break and move while I was trying to find a way across. I saw a small platform of ice in the middle and managed to clamber up on to it with my sledge. Pen and Martin hadn't climbed down on to the moving ice and watched from a large pan of ice as I drifted slowly past them in the middle of a flowing lava of frozen cauliflower soup. Pen later said it looked like I was sailing past them on a majestic boat. Thankfully, it didn't move far or for long and I hopped off on to an adjoining large pan of ice and joined the men again.

During this part of the expedition the sun rose high in the sky and shone on the crystals of the snow, which glittered brightly as we passed by. On day 49 we had our first water crossing. We had brought drysuits for this eventuality but up until then had managed to find a way around open water. The further north we went, the more thin ice and open water there was, and there wasn't always an easy way around. As the navigator and pathfinder it was my job to go first and I donned my big plastic drysuit and climbed into the water, taking my sledge with me, which was made from vacuum-packed Kevlar and so waterproof and buoyant. As I clumsily swam over I began to feel water coming into my suit. I had 50 metres to go when I realized what was happening. I wasn't sure whether to turn back or keep going. I decided to keep pushing on, but more and more water came into the suit. It was truly terrifying. I managed to get to the other side and climbed out. I was frozen solid. I took off the drysuit and emptied the water out. I was both wet and cold, the most dangerous combination in freezing temperatures. I shoved my down jacket on and began to ferociously pull my sledge in large circles to try and get some warmth back in my body while Pen and Martin made the crossing to join me. We set off skiing together but everything hurt from the cold. After constantly pulling the sledge for a while, I could feel the warmth return to my body and felt relieved. We had been given the suits on the last resupply and when we checked them later mine hadn't been sealed along the seams. I was livid for a long time, but eventually you have to let things go.

It was beautiful and clear the next day and we saw a seal for the first time and fox tracks, which made me feel there could be bears around. I hoped we wouldn't have to cross water again, where we would be extremely vulnerable. A large body of water often reflects in the sky and I constantly checked for signs of water up ahead throughout the day. Thankfully, the day ended uneventfully.

Every day in the Arctic is different and on day 51 we woke up to high winds and a storm raging outside. We were tent bound again. We had only five more days until the next resupply so this time, unlike before, it was extremely frustrating. Every day outside was vital now and we felt it strongly when we couldn't move. We spent the day catching up on our diaries, mending kit and hoping the storm would stop so we could begin our duties once more. It was a relief when the next day was still and we could set out once more. The storm had broken up the ice and snowdrifts covered everything, including the thin-ice-covered leads. It was no longer possible to see when we were on thick ice or dangerously thin ice. I probed forward with my pole when I thought I could see undulations in the surface but could never be sure what lay underneath. As I gingerly crossed an uneven patch of ice, my left foot shot through a thin crack and I went into water up to my thigh. Because the crack was thin only my left leg went in and I managed to haul myself out easily. The wind blasted my trouser leg, which froze hard for the next hour. It was uncomfortable but nothing like the difficulties we'd faced in the early days. Everything is relative in the Arctic. We made good mileage and completed all our data gathering despite the difficult soft snow.

The next five days before resupply were fairly uneventful and for me consisted of finding a safe route across the sea ice, which was challenging in itself. There are no maps of the Arctic Ocean, the ice is constantly moving and there are many obstacles in the way. The path is never straight.

On day 56 we found a perfect area for the plane to land, the sky was clear and we had three full days' food left. That evening when we called base we were told that the weather the next day wasn't forecast to be good at Eureka, which is a weather station in the High Arctic and the only civilization between Resolute Bay and ourselves and is where the pilots needed to refuel and rest overnight, as legally they could only fly so many hours, so there would be no resupply the next day. The distance between the airbase at Resolute Bay and us required a stop at Eureka plus one more fuel stop at a depot laid out on the ice earlier, and the next day we were told that the weather wasn't good at the second refuel position and once again would need to be delayed. We now had only two full days' food so decided to go on half rations. The next two days brought us the same news and, as we now had only one day's food and no guarantee of when the resupply would come in, we made the decision to eat as little as possible.

Seven days after that, we were still on the ice with very little food. We were weak and tired but not without hope. We had fuel and knew we could survive for many more days on water. Finally, 11 days after we expected the resupply, the plane came in. The main pilot was Lexy, the first female pilot I had seen on the Arctic Ocean, and I was thrilled that of all the pilots out there it was a woman who came to our aid in such difficult conditions.

As soon as the flight left, we ate until we were stuffed and slept in a warm tent, feeling strong for the final section of the expedition. We didn't know how many days we had left as that depended on the weather and ice conditions, but every day was a day in the beautiful icy world that is the Arctic and as the temperatures had hit –15°C we didn't feel the cold inside or outside the tent. Life was good.

In the end we only had seven more days on the ice. The seasonal break-up of the ice had already begun while we had lain in our sleeping bags waiting so long. The moment we started travelling again we could see the difference. We had many cracks, open water, and a constant patchwork of leads and broken pans to contend with.

Finding a path through the jumbled ice required immense concentration and my eyes strained in the bright sun or the foggy mist that rolled in as we hauled our sledges forward. We continued each day, completing as much research as we could, knowing our days were numbered. All too quickly, our base told us that the ice was breaking up fast and would no longer be safe for a Twin Otter landing if we stayed. Kenn Borek Air, the company that owns the Twin Otters and employs the pilots, needed to get us out and we were given the coordinates of a potential runway to find. Doing my last bit of navigating toward the coordinates of the airstrip was extremely emotional. I was proud of the fact that I'd been up front for 73 days leading the way and had relied on the sun and nature for most of it but I was sad that this would be the last time.

We arrived at our final runway late in the day, pitched our tent and all went outside to do our last scientific duties. We stayed there for just two days and on 13 May, day 75 of the expedition, the Twin Otter came out of the sky and landed to pick us up. David Shukman, the BBC's science editor, climbed out of the plane with his camera crew and we were all interviewed on the ice before heading south, back to civilization.

The Catlin Arctic Survey was received with great acclaim from climate and ice scientists around the world and I was honoured to have been able to do my bit. It was so successful that more scientists wanted to be involved in the next survey, forcing Pen to step out of the field and deal with the organizational side of things. I returned to the ice in the following two years and was an integral part of every expedition.

Before the Catlin Arctic Surveys, I had guided expeditions made up of men, but my big polar expeditions and world records were in all-women teams. This was the first time I had been in a team of Arctic experts as the only woman. I chose to share this story of the first of three Catlin Arctic Surveys rather than the all-women expeditions as they have been well documented and I have shared them many times over. This is the first time I have sat down and told my story of any of the Catlin Arctic Surveys.

Being a woman in an otherwise all-male team was different but just as wonderful. I learned to be confident of my own skills. I didn't need to compete with the guys and insist on pulling a sledge as heavy as theirs, which would have slowed us down. I needed to add my value and my expertise, and by every member of the team doing that we were all equal and a formidable entity.

I can't thank Pen enough for his faith in me. There are not many men out there who would have chosen a woman to lead them physically on the ice. He is a true visionary. And I thank Martin for his great photography work, his friendship, companionship and being there whenever I needed him. Both true gentlemen of steel.

MANGO HAPPY
ANNA McNUFF

Anna McNuff is an adventurer, speaker, bestselling author and self-confessed mischief-maker. She was named by *The Guardian* as one of the top female adventurers of our time and *Condé Nast Traveller* included her in a list of the 50 most influential travellers in the world. She is the UK ambassador for Girlguiding and has swum, cycled and run (sometimes in fancy dress, sometimes in bare feet) over 20,000 miles across the globe. She is relentless in her search for a decent cup of coffee and will never turn down a good slice of lemon pie.

Find out more about Anna at:
W: www.annamcnuff.com
T: @AnnaMcNuff
I: @annamcnuff
F: Anna McNuff

Why take the shortest, most direct route through life when you can take the wiggliest, most mountainous one possible? This was the question that my friend Faye and I asked ourselves when planning a new cycling adventure through South America.

South America had always intrigued me. A mass of wonky teardrop-shaped land way down there, dangling from North America. Clinging on by... well, Panama. I had often wondered what went on down *there* – a land full of desolate sweeping mountain passes, dense jungles, wild and winding rivers, and home to the driest place on earth – the Atacama Desert. Yes, there were drug lords (or so the news told me), but there were also vibrant cities, bottles of delicious wine and many, many llamas. Plus, pop sensation of the early noughties Shakira hailed from South America. She and her hips that don't lie had helped me navigate some turbulent teenage years, so that sealed the deal. South America it would be.

And yet, we needed a twist – some kind of adventuresome goal to get our minds racing and blood pumping before we had even left home. So instead of planning a journey that focused solely on travelling from A to B, we decided to measure ours in the third adventure dimension – upward. Beginning in La Paz, Bolivia, we would shimmy our way 5,500 miles southward, criss-crossing the spine of the Andes mountains, switching between Chile and Argentina, and exploring as many peaks and passes as we could along the way. By the time our journey came to a close at the "end of the world" in Ushuaia, at the tip of South America, we hoped to have ascended over 100,000 metres on humble bicycles.

Landing into La Paz at 4,000 metres above sea level was a baptism of fire. I found it fascinating to learn, for the first time, how my body responded (or rather failed to respond) at altitude. I had high hopes of discovering that we were both specimens of superhumanity – women who could function easily when there was 50 per cent less oxygen in the air than we were used to. Alas, that hope was shattered as we wheezed and spluttered like two geriatric chain-smokers while trying to lift our bikes off the luggage belt. We had come to South America in search of our physical and mental limits, and we reached them at baggage reclaim.

After a period of acclimatization, some short tester rides and wondering for the hundredth time whether we'd bitten off more than we could chew, we felt ready to hit the road. We pedalled out of La Paz, over our first Andean mountain pass and into an area of Bolivian jungle called the Yungas. Now, everybody knows that there are laws in the jungle, and the Yungas was no different. There are two laws that apply in the Yungas – the law of the up and the law of the down. There is no along. Along is a luxury reserved for other areas of Bolivia and something we could only ever dream of while in the Yungas. In fact, a few days into our journey through the area, I began to wonder whether the concept of riding along a horizontal plain was something Faye and I imagined was possible, such was the relentlessness of the ups and the downs.

If you took a bird's-eye view of that area of Bolivia, it would appear as if a giant had scooped up the earth in his palm and crumpled it like a piece of paper. It was all peaks and valleys, highs and lows, deep troughs and gentle summits. Everything in the landscape was green – deep, dark, almost blackish green in places. The only break in the green were the rubble roads, either a yellowish-brown or a dark grey – rising and falling, disappearing around bends, flowing onward into the horizon and mirroring the path of the dark green rivers that weaved along the valley floor, way down below. If it was a hot, dry day then those roads coated us in dust, every spare particle of it clinging to our glistening skin or sweat-sodden clothing. If it was a rainy day, as happened often in the Yungas, the roads would grow thick muddy fingers and take hold of our tyres, sucking our bikes into the earth, clawing as we passed, slowing progress from a few miles an hour to not much at all.

Each morning, over a breakfast of crackers and cheese outside our tents, Faye would call over to me:

"How many metres are we in for today, McNuff?" to which my reply would usually detail a number between 1,500 and 3,500 metres. Those metres were usually split between two or three big climbs over the course of the day, so Faye would get a briefing on that, too. We rarely spoke about distance. Distance became irrelevant in the Yungas – the Land of No Along.

We soon came up with a strategy to break up the long climbs and decided to stop for a short break every time we gained 100 metres in altitude. A 100-metre upward stint would usually take us 20 minutes of cycling, which doesn't sound like long, but when the temperature is between 35–41°C, there's 80 per cent humidity and you're grappling for balance on a rocky trail, then 20 minutes is long enough. We found that we could just about bear the exertion for those 20 minutes before needing to flop into the shade at the side of the road and throw as much water down our necks as we could.

Had you looked at our route for the first week of our journey through the Yungas, you would have been forgiven for thinking that someone had let a child loose with an Etch A Sketch. It zigged and it zagged, and then it zagged some more – making its way through the small villages of Coscoma, Coripata, Auquisamaña, Parani, Machacamarca and Los Anguias, each with a population of no more than 100 people and often fewer. As we passed through each village, we were chased by dogs, cheered on by children playing in the street and we swerved around brave, wild chickens (who were actually trying to cross the road).

These villages served as neat little markers to break up the long, hot days in the saddle. Each small pocket of civilisation was different to the last and we never knew what we would find. Many were just a few streets wide, with small concrete houses and tin roofs, the walls left grey and unpainted. Others were larger, with plazas (town squares) surrounded by houses with whitewashed walls.

The plazas were my favourite places to take a rest. When I struggled on the bike, I looked forward to each one, collecting them and the people who lived around them like trinkets. Some plazas would boast grand statues, lines of trees, flowerbeds, pagodas with vines and varnished wooden benches. Others were more modest – empty, dusty squares with concrete benches around the edge and an open gazebo at one end, which offered respite from the midday sun. Whatever the plaza's size, there was always an explosion of activity, of colour, of noise. Street corners shrouded in the giggles of teenage girls, who were dressed in jeans and bright T-shirts, with jet black hair running down their backs. Younger kids kicked footballs around, shrieking with delight. I'd catch wafts of boiled meat and potatoes escaping from the houses, swiftly followed by the whiff of a nearby pile of rubbish, which had been left out in the sun on the curb just that little bit too long. These plazas were a window to a secret world and they epitomized what we had come to know about Bolivia. Vast stretches of nothingness on a harsh dusty road and then, just around the bend, there everybody was.

As the days wore on in the Yungas, and we creaked and groaned deeper into the jungle, these towns became our lifelines. Much as we both loved the solitude on the roads in between them, I craved the shot glass full of civilisation that they served up. It was always just enough to fuel us for the next stint. It's not something we ever spoke about, but I had a feeling that Faye felt the same. Whenever we lay on plaza benches, in the shade of a nearby tree, drinking in the scene going on around us, neither one of us was in a rush to leave.

The morning we left our camp spot in the hills above the village of Arapata, our tyres jostled for position on an especially uneven and loose road surface. Riding our bikes downhill was like clinging on to a pneumatic drill. Our hands juddered on the handlebars, our arms shook, all of our wobbly bits jiggled and if we didn't clamp our teeth tightly together, they would chatter all the way down too. It was on these long downhills, which sometimes lasted for up to 90 minutes, that I wondered whether I perhaps preferred slogging uphill. But on the ups I wished to go down, and on the downs I wished I was going up. It was modern life all over – the grass was always greener on the other side of the hill in the Yungas.

At the bottom of the valley, I had just about regained some feeling in my hands and eased off on the brakes when I noticed a strong smell in the air.

"Faye... can you smell that?" I sniffed.

"Smell what?" she said.

"I'm not sure... it smells like home brew? Like rotting fruit?" I replied, now looking off to the side of the road and into the trees. Faye spotted them before I did.

"MANGOOOOSSS!!!" she hollered at the top of her lungs.

"MANGOOOSSSS!!" I hollered back.

And there they were – hundreds of mango trees lining the roadside, laid out in rows with big juicy green teardrop-shaped things dripping from every branch. Now, I'd never been anywhere that mangos grow before, and what with them being in my top three favourite fruits of all time (the mighty banana will never be beaten and the blueberry sneaks a close second), I was overcome with excitement. It was like meeting a pop star. I'd been a big fan of mangos and their work in my local supermarket for many years now, but to see them in the flesh, on their home turf, hanging around naturally in the trees – well, that was fabulous. I inhaled a long, deep breath and let the hot mango-tinged air hit the back of my throat.

We pedalled on, riding along the valley floor in dappled sunlight. Soon we passed some modest terracotta-coloured homes, where I watched the residents picking the fruit and piling it into large orange crates. I liked being able to see what they did in that town. These were the mango people and everyone had a job. While the pickers picked, others shovelled unripened fruit under large green plastic sheets to warm in the sun. One man who was stood next to a rusty blue 4x4 truck handed crates of mangos to his two young kids, before driving off with both the children and fruit piled precariously on the open back.

On the outskirts of the mango town, I could bear it no longer. Pulling over at the side of the road, I spotted some trees that didn't look like they were part of anyone's orchard. I lay the bike gently down on the ground and darted up the bank. After plucking two ripe-looking mangos from a tree, I returned to Faye and handed her one of them.

"Care for a mango m'lady Faye?" I offered in a faux posh voice.

"Oooo. Why thank you. Don't mind if I do," she replied.

Our grubby little fingers couldn't peel back the skin fast enough and, after several agonizing moments, I plunged the whole thing into my gob. Sucking the orange flesh from around the stone, mango juice dribbled down my chin and on to my hands. It was sweet, it was sticky and it was deeee-licious.

As is the rule with sweet, sticky and delicious things, one mango leads to two mangos, leads to three mangos... and more. Twenty minutes later we were still in the vice-like grip of the mango grove, repeatedly scrambling up the banks and gobbling from the trees like wild animals. I pulled out my phone and took a video, to make sure I would never forget the moment I ate my first wild mango: "We cannot leave the mango area!" I shouted. "I have mango stuck in my teeth, it's all over my hands. I have mango on my face. We are mango happy!"

Eventually, we managed to drag ourselves away from the mango groves and continue on down the valley. By that point it was approaching midday and the temperature had started to soar. Now coated in a mix of mango juice, sweat and dust, we looked an absolute state. As we crossed a small river, I glanced down at the clear rushing water. It looked so cool and fresh, tumbling over rocks and whooshing under the small wooden bridge beneath our wheels. I looked at Faye, then back to the river. We didn't even need to exchange words, she knew exactly what I was thinking. I followed as she turned right down a small track to the river's edge. We hopped off the bikes and waded straight into the river, fully clothed. I let out a little yelp as the icy water hit my ankles, then calves, thighs and then that no-going-back moment... the crotch. Soon I was in for a full-body dunk. Oh, the relief! After a minute or so in the water, I headed back to my bike to grab my camera. When I turned back around, Faye was sat waist deep in the water, just on the edge of the river. She was looking out upstream with a huge grin on her face. I took a photo of her through the blades of long green grass that lined the bank. She was easily visible in her blue T-shirt against a backdrop of green, smiling from ear to ear. Despite the mango gorging, I noticed how her face was gaunt, far slimmer than it had been when we arrived in La Paz a few weeks earlier. She looked so happy there – her auburn hair plastered to her cheeks, waist deep in an icy stream in the middle of the Bolivian jungle.

Soon, I rejoined Faye in the river. Sitting beside her with the water rushing over my legs, I took in a deep breath and exhaled. Despite the hardships, the slow progress, the stifling heat and the new addition of biting bugs, the Yungas had begun to enchant me. I had never been anywhere like it, let alone had the privilege to ride a bike through somewhere like that. And that's exactly what it felt like – a privilege. The landscape was so dense. It was dripping with vegetation, birds and bugs – like it should be somewhere only reserved for travelling by foot. With each mile that passed there it felt as if the thick layers of bush had parted to allow us through and then closed up behind us, like a magic maze. In the Yungas we were not looking out on the landscape, we were in it. We were riding through it, entangled in the branches of its trees and swept along by its meandering rivers until such a time came that it wanted to release us back to the real world.

———

It's hard to explain the kind of freedom that a journey by bike can bring. Being able to camp wherever you please each night, and waking at dawn to be greeted by a new and different view; sunlight streaming through a pine forest, the morning mist rising over a *laguna*, cacti perched precariously on red rocks, a glacier snaking down a granite peak, stumbling unexpectedly across a grove of mangos. There's a deep sense of fulfilment that comes from moving through ever-changing landscapes, with everything you need to survive balanced between a frame and two wheels, and knowing that the only person who can propel you onward is you. Truth be told, the vast unknowing of an adventure is so ill at odds with the comfort and safety of modern life that it's daunting. I'll never get used to the feeling of throwing myself in at the deep end and wondering whether I'm in over my head. But a willingness to be vulnerable will always breed strength. And I'm not talking the kind of flex-yer-muscles, "let's go do some deadlifts bro" kind of strength. I mean an inner strength. A strength that only you can see. One built through the simple joy of managing to keep the pedals turning, even when the road ahead is steep and you're always gasping for breath.

WHERE THE MUSK OXEN ROAM

ANNIE LLOYD-EVANS

Annie Lloyd-Evans is a Scottish outdoor woman. Fuelled by curiosity, tea and big empty spaces, she is often found staring longingly at maps. By day she tries to inspire young people to challenge themselves outdoors, and by night she dreams up her own adventures far and wide.

After spending a few years hitch-hiking around Europe, Annie started cycle touring and bike-packing. She has ridden solo through France and Taiwan and ridden technical mountain bike tours on the Tour du Mont Blanc and Haute Route in the Alps, alongside many shorter routes in the Scottish Highlands.

Since then, Annie and her partner have ridden through Iceland, Patagonia and Nepal and branched into winter fat biking, crossing Iceland in the depths of winter and following ski trails in the Swedish Arctic. Having added a packraft to her adventure toolbox, she has been exploring new routes in Scotland by bike and boat and completed a three-week-long, self-sufficient bike-rafting wilderness journey in Greenland.

Find out more about Annie at:
W: annieleoutside.com
I: @a_girl_outside

Water stretches away on all sides, the surface a dull green and gently rippled by the breeze. Huge, grey cliffs rise almost 1,000 metres vertically, looming ahead. Runnels of scree glint in the last rays of sun, clouds lowering just enough to veil the small ice cap. I'm floating in a packraft (a small inflatable boat) with my fat bike (a type of bicycle specially designed with larger than usual tyres to enable it to travel over rough ground) strapped to the front, in the middle of a 4-kilometre crossing of the fjord. This is probably the most dangerous part of our whole expedition. Our trip involves packrafting some 90 kilometres down a sea fjord to gain access to a huge valley system. We are hoping that once there, we'll be able to ride our bikes along the twisting corridor through the snow-capped hills back east, toward our starting point.

As the evening light starts to deepen, and the clouds build, my instinct is to paddle hard, not stopping until I am in the safety of the rocky shoreline opposite. Huw paddles slower than me though, and he has fallen behind. I wait impatiently, trying to focus on the beauty of this place, to enjoy and take in this feeling of incredible vulnerability. It is not something we experience often, that total overwhelming realization that we are at the mercy of the weather out here, in one of the longest fjords in Greenland. There really is no one to hear you scream. We would not be the first to disappear on this body of water.

The cries and wails of a loon echo off the cliffs as we reach the cool shade of the far side. These birds are one of the few signs of life; their call is eerie and unsettling. The wind has changed direction and strengthened – we are now battling into a headwind. Another 15 minutes and we have to abandon the water, scrambling awkwardly up the rocks with our heavy loads. Though this spot is far from perfect, we manage to get the tent pitched on a tiny, sloping, boggy platform. The view out to an impressive sharp, arrow-headed peak helps to take my mind away from the thought that the wind could toss our things over the edge and right into the milky water. As white caps rage on the sea below, it is with great relief that we sip our tea from our slightly squelchy perch. Tomorrow we will paddle the remaining few kilometres to the start of our valley system, where we will switch transport modes, rolling up the packrafts and assembling our bicycles.

The crossing done, we have time to reflect on our last few days at sea. The fjord, a long arm of sea that reaches far inland, surrounded by huge granite cliffs, had thrown us many challenges. Paddling with the tides has meant some early starts and late-night finishes. The constant worry over what is to come has been exhausting. Being far less experienced paddlers than we are pedallers, we had to escape the fjord several times with increasing winds, often dragging our laden boats up steep, slippery rocks out of the reach of the waves. Among all this, there is a peace that comes from having to connect with nature to such a degree, reading the weather and accepting we cannot always push on. Being stuck for 36 hours while the wind raged gave us an opportunity to fish, collect berries and scramble about on the beautiful rocky outcrops. Still, it will be with a sense of relief when we can exchange the uncertainty of the water for solid ground.

A few days later, we find ourselves reaching the entrance to the valley system we plan to follow for the next week. We have examined satellite imagery of every bend and zoomed in on the river's meanders to see if there is any way round. Yet despite those hours of research, there is no real answer, no guarantee that it would be rideable. We really are heading into the unknown. It is on my twenty-ninth birthday that we push over a terminal moraine, the final obstacle to the valley, and get our first view ahead. We start laughing, crying; the valley stretches ahead, a huge, ice-scoured corridor, outwash plains lining the sides of the roaring glacial river. It's everything we had hoped for, imagined and dreamed of as we sweated, pushed and doubted the past week. Getting here has not been easy, what with battling gales on the water, waves washing over the boats, getting stormbound with no fresh water, and carrying bikes loaded with around 40 kilograms of kit and food over some very steep, loose scree. Now, finally, it seems the gamble may have paid off.

Riding down the far side of the moraine, we link up with caribou trails until we reach the desert below – this is a totally unexpected phenomenon in the middle of a land created by ice. This unexpected nature of the land repeated itself over and over on our journey, the worries of going somewhere so unknown eclipsed by the delight and joy in discovering it for ourselves. The fine grey sands reach to the horizon, punctuated only by huge erratic boulders, some as big as houses. As I ride, my vision seems to blur and the rock ahead shifts slightly – I'm tired. I blink and keep pedalling. The rock moves again.

Then splits into two, one big, one small. This time my eyes are not lying: the mama and baby musk ox stare at me, equally as fascinated by us as we are by them. The clear light glints off their snowy muzzles and short white legs, which are just visible, poking from underneath their magnificent woollen gowns. We are about 50 metres apart, and once my initial intrigue wears off, I realize that that is not very far, and, as huggable as she looks, that mama might decide she doesn't want her baby getting mixed up in bad company. Also, she has an impressive pair of not-very-cuddly-looking curved horns. Just as I am starting to back away, she turns tail and leads her little one to a high vantage point, her huge coat sashaying as she gallops.

We camp that night by the first water we find, a tiny stream pioneering a path through the sands, lined by a bright green dusting of shrubs and marram grass. We pitch on the firmest patch of sand we can find, hoping to prove the words of Matthew in the Bible wrong. As we watch the sunset from a rocky outcrop several hundred metres above our tent, we get our first warning signs. In the distance enormous clouds of sand are streaming across our trail from earlier – our tracks will be obliterated before sundown. Huge katabatic gusts of wind are falling from the ice sheet above, tearing down into our valley. For now, we are in the lee of it.

At 4 a.m. the tent is ripped out of the ground. Sand is everywhere, sticking to my bare skin. I'm out in the predawn light while Huw attempts to hold the tent down from the inside. For the next half hour we scurry about in our pants, gathering the heaviest rocks we can carry to stack on to the pegs. Crawling back into the tent, we hope the worst is over. Lying in the faint light, staring at the thin Dyneema fabric whooshing and sucking, the wind occasionally lifting and pulling upward, we know there will be no more sleep tonight.

The wind continues into the next day and, as we ride on up the valley, sand is flung hard into our faces and stray gusts knock us off our bikes. We are riding over smoothed rocks, lumpy awkward ground that is difficult on the heavy bikes. There is no easy spinning here. Lack of sleep catches up with us as we try to cross a river – halfway across and we realize it's deeper and faster than we thought. The water clutches at the wheels, pulling and dragging them from us. It's a tenuous retreat back to our side, and as the rain begins to fall, we resign ourselves to a much longer trudge in the narrow margin between river and cliff. Eventually we give in, and inflate the boats for the short crossing on a calmer meander. Once on the other side, the land is open, flat. The valley splits ahead; a huge cliff face rises up at the divide. We stay left, following the freshwater river, with its gloriously clear water. It's nice to leave behind the roar of the dark, messy glacial river.

Our valley is huge, maybe a kilometre across, with the sheer sides reaching upward in colours of orange, red and silver stripes. The ground is covered in a beautiful green; the tops of the grass tinged yellow as autumn is fast approaching. Dwarf willow grows in sheltered hollows and hugs the cliff base. At one point we have to drag our bikes through a mini forest of these tightly growing trees, worrying about ripping our derailleurs off. Strands of snagged wool blow in the wind like creamy streamers. The musk oxen population is extremely dense and they have created wonderful, organically winding trails that we follow. Our journey is often interrupted to observe these tawny creatures and one morning we watch three young males tear about, before charging at each other, heads meeting in huge clashes, the sound echoing all around off the valley walls. The rut won't begin for another few weeks, which we are grateful for – as much as these animals are cautious of us, there have been numerous accounts of the males being very aggressive during mating season.

As we move higher up the valley, the corridor narrows and we arrive at a squeeze. The rock must be different here, too hard to have been pulverized by the ice. There is no obvious choice, no easy route. We follow the most trodden ox trails and weave through boulders, pushing up steep slopes and passing bikes to each other to get by. We have no idea if this will improve – our map, with its enormous 1:350,000 scale, suggests that it will widen again ahead. We can only keep moving and hope.

High-pitched squeals draw us out of our trudge: above, two juvenile eagles play and practise in the air. Constantly swooping over one another, and squeaking, it seems as though they are goading each other into feats of greater daring. We watch them, squinting against the sun, until they spiral upward and out of sight. Just as our energy is dwindling, we crest the hill we have been sweating, swearing and pushing over. In the moment that it takes to process the view, we know it has been worth it. On long, remote expeditions the highs are so high: laughing out loud, crying, jumping around in happiness and relief that things are working. The river ahead is wide, slow, reflecting azure in the afternoon sun. Directly below us it passes through the gorge we have been pushing through; bright green pondweed waves gently in the current, the water clear right down to its rocky bed. In deeper pools we can see Arctic char, lazily wagging their tails as they face upstream. This is perfection.

Camping on a dry patch, we call our first early finish. After nearly two weeks of hard work it's a joy to laze in the sun, paddle about and play on the crystal river and watch a few lone musk oxen while drinking endless cups of tea. We both attempt our first wash and scrub our shorts. I love moments like this, when you are at peace, and can just sit still and absorb the surroundings. We listen to the ravens nesting on the cliff opposite as they chat and bicker like any married couple, watch the damselflies as they flit about like jewels. A time out from thinking about what is next. Huw fishes, catching himself some gratefully received extra nutrition. The char are beautiful: delicately spotted with colour running from deep silver to a warm sunset orange on the belly. Often on trips I feel like there is never enough time to totally appreciate the land – that my mind needs a pause. Stopping for a few hours allows it to catch up and for the land to embed itself in me.

For the next day or so, we keep working up the valley. Now out of the protected area, signs of hunting and old human habitation are everywhere. We pass circles of musk oxen heads, the whole family shot as they clustered protectively around their young. We have mixed feelings about it, although we know this land is a resource for the native Greenlanders – has been for centuries, and will be well after we are gone. It is still sad to see. The old stone circles and accompanying midden piles remind us that we are just sightseers in this land, and our touristic judgement is not useful here.

In the distance we see a male caribou. He's strutting his stuff, head high, antlers back, and tiptoeing around as though on hot coals. Then he changes course and charges right at us. Taken aback, we just stop and stare stupidly as the clatter of hooves and dust draw close. A huge snort, a skidded stop, 2 metres from us, and he storms off in a fluster. We think he has gone but then he pops back over a small rise and prances around us before urinating heavily right in front of us. It seems clear that he is displeased with our presence and is telling us in the loudest and smelliest way possible.

Once again we must work with the tides. Our final few days will take us out of an arm of the fjord and back across to the harbour where it all began. Unfortunately for us, our idea of tides – flowing one way when it's coming in, the other when it's going out – turns out to be oversimplified. Add in branches off the main fjord and some very powerful glacial river water flowing in, and the result is a confusing mass of water fighting with itself. After several frustrating hours paddling into a strong current and then sitting waiting for it to weaken, we make it around some huge banded cliffs into the main fjord. The sun is low, and with the stillness it is beautiful. The water reflects the warmth of the sky and although we know dusk is descending fast, we don't rush. Huge cliffs line the fjord here – there is nowhere obvious where we can camp.

A few kilometres ahead there's a gentler mound sticking out from the main wall and we aim for that. It's deep dusk as we arrive, and there is no easy place to get off here as steep, slippery rocks rise 5 metres out of the water. I jump off, underestimating the gradient. Unstrapping the bicycle from the packraft, I attempt to carry both up the steep slope. I lose control and the packraft slides down and shoots off into the sea. I feel so stupid! I teeter on a small ledge, clinging on to my bike so that it doesn't follow my boat down into the water. But even my bike is still too heavy for me to drag up to the first big ledge so I am just stuck, with only my toes on a flat step. Fortunately, Huw is just approaching and tows my boat back. I'm standing on the only small step though, and as he steps on to the wet rock he slips right into the freezing water with his heavy rucksack on. I can't even move to help, and it is with much relief that he scrabbles his way out. With silent rage he helps me shuttle all our kit up, and in silence we trudge for what feels like a long way to find somewhere flat. This spot is clearly an access point for the local hunters – we step around rotting entrails and are put off the first spot by the fly-infested head and legs of a perished musk ox.

Forcing Huw to put on all my warm clothes, I set up the tent and get the stove on. It's been one of the longest, more frustrating days of our trip and tomorrow our journey will be over. I sit in the darkness, looking out over the fjord, the lights of an enormous cruise ship glowing like some weird deep-sea jellyfish. The end of a trip is always hard. We have been out on unpathed, empty land for over two weeks. Tomorrow will bring all the luxuries of a human settlement: big sticky pastries, litres of sweet drinking yoghurt and big plates of cooked food. With that of course comes all the downsides: the scummy water of the harbour, busloads of Danish pensioners photographing us, and having to pay to camp in an overcrowded, dirty spot with no view. Returning is always a jolt.

This is one of the first places we have travelled through that feels wild. Of course, humans do impact the land – the Greenlanders come inland for a couple of months to hunt – but their presence is small as everything they kill must be carried out under human power. It is quite an incredible sight. To be so close to the huge ice cap, on land that is still relatively young and yet full of life, is glorious. The tiny, fragile flowers seem so frail next to the bare rocks. Wildlife is abundant, and strikingly present. It seems to want to show off everything it has during the short summer season, glowing with health and vigour. Hares skip among the scree, char gather fearlessly in the river, and high above us eagles soar, looking down on the dusting of musk oxen and caribou herds. It is humbling to be here, and for a very brief moment to exist alongside a place so innocent of all humankind's shortcomings.

WHY ME?
ANOUSHÉ HUSAIN

Anoushé Husain is a champion for all those experiencing barriers and self-limiting beliefs, sharing her journey to help others unlock their potential.

Born missing her right arm below the elbow, living with multiple health conditions, a cancer survivor, a Muslim and coming from an ethnic minority, Anoushé has never let what society or culture thinks she should do limit her or dictate the direction of her life. She is constantly breaking the mould and challenging not only her own beliefs about her potential but also those of society and her own culture.

Anoushé candidly talks about her life, how she has remained resilient in the face of huge obstacles and talks about issues that we as a society do not talk about enough. In particular, Anoushé highlights the plight of those stigmatized by society in order to change the misconceptions around these groups.

A civil servant by day, Anoushé is a paraclimber in the UK and co-founder of Paraclimbing London as well as an ambassador for both Ehlers-Danlos Support UK and LimbPower, the leading charity for amputees and those with limb difference. She also supports the Grit&Rock Foundation, which aims to help teenage girls aged 13–15 from deprived, inner-city backgrounds develop greater grit, determination and self-confidence.

Find out more about Anoushé at:

W: www.anoushehusain.com

T: @AnousheHusain

I: @anoushehusain

F: @AnousheHusain1

Why me? What did I do to deserve this?
I can't do this any more.

Those were the three things I thought to myself as my doctor told me I had cancer.

At 24, I was facing a cancer diagnosis. It had arrived out of the blue, discovered by accident. My life, already complicated by health issues, was about to get far more complex. This wasn't the life I always had. Sure, as a child, I was poorly, and yes, I was born with my right arm missing below the elbow and had a few other issues that had been corrected surgically, but I was also a sporty kid. I competed in swimming and then found Shotokan karate, a sport that I invested a lot of my time in as a teenager. Sport has always been an escape for me, a sanctuary from whatever stress is going on in life. That is, until my body started to fail me.

Around the age of 14, my joints began to slip out of their sockets. It was painful in the beginning, but I also thought it was a pretty awesome party trick. I showed my parents one day and, sadly, they, along with my medical team, didn't see it the same way as me. I was put into physiotherapy. No one knew why my joints were being weird. The term "hypermobile" was mentioned a lot and everyone said it would be fine.

Two years later, not only had we seen no progress in my more degraded joints, but other unaffected joints were now following suit. By then, I was practising karate 16 hours a week. It was my lifeline, helping me to cope between hard studies and feeling like I didn't fit in very well at school. I am visibly different and I was one of the few people in my school from an ethnic minority and a Muslim. Given the geopolitical climate of the time, it's hardly surprising that I was targeted by bullies. I had had issues in karate too – in this case, discrimination based on the fact that I had a visible disability. I was banned from competitions and forced to remain in the beginner classes in an attempt to demotivate me and prompt me to quit. I was also ignored in classes by the head coach. But I stuck with the sport and told no one, just so that I could keep practising. Thankfully, an amazing coach who is still my friend today spotted the discrimination and got me back into competition.

Six weeks after being allowed to compete again, I lost in the first round of my first competition to the champion of Switzerland. My team stood around me, comforting me for the thrashing I received. I was just happy. Happy to have competed, proud that I could say I lost to the champion of Switzerland (how cool is that?!) and thankful that, for once, I was being treated the same as everyone else.

The next year, I won my first podium position and that same week I was in discussions about joining the national team. Three days after that came a bombshell. The surgeon I had been consulting about my joint problems said that due to the lack of progress I had to stop karate. I wasn't even allowed to have a last training session, just to say goodbye. I went to my club and met with the head coach (the one responsible for my difficulties at the club) and told him I had to stop karate. His response was a joyous smile – I was finally out of his hair. As I left to go home that afternoon, my heart broke. That same year, I took a break from completing my Duke of Edinburgh Gold Award. I had completed bronze and silver, but my medical team thought it was going to be too much for me to finish the gold at that point in time.

To say that the next few years were difficult is probably an understatement. I had lost the first love of my life and no matter what sport I tried to replace it with – and I tried loads – nothing worked. To make matters worse, there was an unintended consequence of stopping karate. While the intention of stopping was to prevent my joints from getting looser, they actually got much worse. By the time I was 18, I had to have surgery on my thumb, which left me completely dependent on family for personal care during the summer when I finished secondary school and was getting ready for university. At 20, I was in surgery again, but I was also fighting to keep my life as normal as possible. I was doing OK in my first degree at university, preparing to go for a six-month exchange to China and getting really excited about the expedition for my Duke of Edinburgh Gold Award in the Pyrenees.

My relationship with my body had got quite bad. My health issues meant that I was less active and I had started to gain weight. I had also developed thyroid issues, exacerbating the weight gain and causing fatigue. I had lost a lot of the physical fitness I had in my karate days. I was allowed to do my expedition but wasn't fit enough to carry a backpack any more. I was still happy to go, but it was dawning on me that this unknown joint condition was starting to disable me. It was already scaring me. I was fighting this unknown thing and my body just wasn't good enough to do the job. I stopped trusting my body. I stopped listening to the signals she was giving me and I was unforgiving when she failed.

The trip to the Pyrenees was amazing. I struggled, but it felt so good to be pushing myself to my physical limits, just walking the paths, one step after another, with no other thoughts. My friends who had already finished their gold told me that when I was ready to finish mine they would come with me. I would never have finished my gold without them. After three gruelling days in the mountains, we walked back to base camp. I needed to get something out of one of the cars and I remember feeling a sharp pain in my back as I tried to pull the car door handle. I didn't know it then, but two discs in my back had slipped. A week later, when I was back home, I started to limp and felt pain radiating down my right leg.

Over the next year, my ability to walk became increasingly compromised. The pain just would not go away. I finished my bachelor's degree in translation studies and took a year off to focus on studying other languages, unsure of where I wanted to go next. I had a place waiting for me at Warwick to study international relations or a place at the University of Luxembourg to study European governance. Both degrees looked amazing. I went for the course in Luxembourg, partly because I thought it would be more relevant to what I wanted to do later, but also because I could go back to living at home with my parents. My health had deteriorated and I couldn't really imagine not having the use of a car or having to manage my own life totally independently. I was also scheduled to have back surgery to fix the issues with my discs.

At 23, I started my master's degree. I was excited to be there, but I was also walking around with electrodes stuck to my back to numb the pain long enough that I could sit through lectures.

I was scared to move because of the pain and in more pain because I wasn't moving. It was an awful catch-22 situation in which many people with chronic pain find themselves. The surgeon put me through an extra set of scans because I was healing so slowly from the back surgery. That was when they spotted a tumour. "It's definitely benign," my consultant told me, "but we will keep an eye on it. If it grows more then it's still aggressive and we should take it out." Six months later, it was nearly triple the size. It had to come out. The surgery was meant to be on Friday 13 May, and while I'm not superstitious, I'm relieved the doctor postponed until 17 May.

A couple of weeks later, I was at a university class party to celebrate the end of classes for that year when I got the call from the hospital. They confirmed that my tumour was benign. I sighed in relief and thought to myself that maybe now I could finally start moving away from the medical drama that my life had become. I felt positive. It was a new year, and I had just turned 24.

It was a Thursday morning and I was sitting on the sofa working out what my dissertation topic would be when the phone rang. It was the secretary at the hospital, asking if I could come in on Saturday. The doctor needed to check the surgery site. All routine, I thought – the doctor must be heading off on holiday and wants to get through all his patients before he goes. Call me naive or glass half full, but I genuinely thought that going into a hospital on a Saturday for an unscheduled appointment was normal...

That Saturday was sunny. Mum was abroad visiting my grandparents, who were in the US at the time. Dad was gardening. I went to the hospital on my own. In hindsight, nothing about that day was normal. The doctor was in his "civilian" clothes and the hospital's outpatients area had been opened specifically for me. There was no one else in the building.

He called me in, smiling but serious, and told me quite calmly, "We found anomalous cells in your tumour."

"Anomalous cells?" I replied, while thinking in my head: *Who says that? What does that mean? Oh wait, not normal cells... oh no.*

"Yes, anomalous cells. We thought your tumour was benign, but we found anomalous cells," he continued.

My head was in a whirl. I knew what he was trying to say, but he wasn't saying the word. He wasn't saying that word that strikes fear through anyone who hears it.

"You mean cancer."

"Yes, anomalous cells."

"No, you have to say it's cancer. If you want me to believe it, you have to use the C-word."

"You have cancer."

I had been fighting so hard to get my body back on track after every setback over the previous ten years that when the doctor told me I had cancer I honestly didn't know how I was going to do it. I felt like I was already at rock bottom. How could I survive yet another blow? Not just another blow like a surgery, but an actual cancer diagnosis... The rest of the appointment went in a blur. I was scheduled for surgery a week later and then I was going to go through a battery of scans and tests to see if and how far it had spread. So I had a week to get my life in order.

I don't remember driving home but I do remember telling my dad in the garden what had happened. It's probably the only time I've ever heard him swear. I sent an email to the university to tell them I had a diagnosis but no idea what my treatment plan was going to be. Then there were appointments with my doctors. Mum was still abroad at the time, so while things were quite real, they weren't totally real yet.

That week was horrific. I was reading all the research that I could find online, freaking out and asking myself: *Why me? What did I do?* I met with one of my doctors, who told me I had got cancer because I wasn't happy enough in life. She definitely reinforced the thought that things were my fault. Not something one needs to hear when one is distraught. This was also the time when I decided that only very close family and friends would find out I had cancer. I wasn't mentally or emotionally prepared to deal with the questions, other people's worries or the implied judgement that I had done something wrong to deserve my cancer. In fact, it took five years for me to decide to come out publically about my cancer. This meant I was dealing with an "invisible" illness (I was wearing a headscarf and wearing fake eyelashes so I was hiding it pretty well) in an incredibly isolated way. I also didn't know any people my age who had cancer.

After I had my follow-up surgery, Mum arrived back and started coming with me to appointments. Then the time came for me to meet my oncologist. I saw three doctors that day. My GP, who said she knew my oncologist and that I'd never get chemo from her. My surgeon, who said my prognosis was so good that I was probably going to get away with radiotherapy or maybe even no treatment.

When I got to my oncologist, I went into the room on my own and she asked me, "Are you a direct person or someone who beats around the bush?"

In my head I knew if she was asking me that, it meant she had something awful to say. "Give it to me," I said.

"I like your style," she replied.

Words can't really describe the next 45 minutes but I went from *why me?* mode to *I have no choice but to sit and accept what is happening. I'm going to have to do this – not fight it, just survive it.*

Two more surgeries, five months of chemo, a month of radiotherapy and tablets I still take to this day. I broke. If I had broken physically with the decline in my health due to the unnamed joint issues causing my body to fail, I broke emotionally with the cancer. This wasn't my body failing due to a condition attacking me – this was my body attacking itself from the inside out. I had failed her. I had failed. I lost my motivation to make physical gains. What was the point? Something was going to go wrong again. Chemo was wrecking my body and spirit. But the hospital was there to support me. They put me into a supervized gym programme as I couldn't get up a single flight of stairs any more and I was struggling to walk more than a few minutes without stopping due to fatigue or pain. Another side effect of my surgeries was that I was having mobility issues. I couldn't reach above my head for very long, and I hadn't recovered well from my other surgeries. This was starting to seriously impair my independence: showering, washing my hair, getting dressed... I was struggling with grip and with strength.

Once the main part of my treatment was complete, I started to rebuild my body. In the beginning, a few minutes of walking on a flat surface was a challenge. With time, walking got easier, and a few months later I managed my first 10-kilometre walk and started working full-time. The hand and arm issues hadn't resolved themselves – if anything, my scars were starting to stiffen and it was getting harder to maintain what mobility was left in my left arm. That was when one of my best friends who came with me on my gold DofE expedition suggested I go climbing with her, to see if the movement would help my arm.

I had tried climbing on a school trip as an eight-year-old and didn't think much of it – at the time, I was a regular competitive swimmer. When I tried the climb, I got up half a route, enjoyed the experience, but I didn't think it was anything special. When we went back on the same trip with school the next year, I was determined to top the wall, and I did it. That sense of satisfaction stuck with me. My parents thought climbing was a dangerous sport, but it was something I wanted to do. I never thought it would be something I would take up after having gone through cancer treatment, especially with my left arm the way it was. I still hadn't found something to replace karate, and that part of my heart was still grieving. I thought my friend was nuts to suggest it! How was I going to tighten my harness? Tie a knot? Grip the holds and pull myself up?

My friend suggested I was scared and said something that has stuck with me: "What have you got to lose? What's the worst that can happen? The best is that you find something you love; at worst, you'll know it didn't work."

Her argument was enough to persuade me to try climbing with her.

The session was awful. I was terrified but I also couldn't get up any routes. A few moves and I was on the floor exhausted. But there were a very few precious seconds when I was balancing on the wall, trying to make progress, when I forgot how despairing my life had become. I escaped. For the first time in ages, I felt like a normal person and it was that feeling that kept me coming back to climb. I would go every few months

Why Me? Anoushé Husain

with my friend to climb, and I kept going to the gym to regain physical fitness.

I was pretty much just about reaching the top of the most basic wall by the time I moved to London for work in 2013. When I moved to London, I took some time to work on who I'd become. It was the first real chance I'd had to feel into what cancer had done to me – or, rather, how I was going to move on from it. I went from *why me?* to *what can I do about it?* The situation might be entirely awful, but ultimately I have the choice about how I react and what I take from it. From this, my mantra developed, a mantra that was very different to my previous way of seeing life and my body:

I am who I am.
I trust my body.
She will take me where I want to go.
Wherever that may be.
I know I will be OK.
I have chosen to trust, to commit, to live
the journey as it reveals itself.
I own and accept the process, outcomes and consequences.
Whatever they may be.

For the first two years in London, I stopped climbing. When life settled down a bit, I realized I missed climbing every few months as I had done in Luxembourg and I wanted to go more frequently. I moved into a new flat at the end of 2015, and that was when my flatmate and I decided to go and be bad at climbing together. It was around then that I heard that

83

in the UK there are national competitions for paraclimbers (climbers with disabilities and/or long-term health conditions). I had never competed as a para athlete and I hadn't trained in a sport in well over ten years, but the match had been lit in my heart. I wanted to see what would happen if I asked my body to train again.

In February 2016, I got a coach. I went from climbing every few months to every few weeks, then to weekly by the end of that year. In my first competition season, I ranked second in the UK in my category and third the year after. Around the same time, I started blogging about my experiences, my medical issues including cancer, the fears I have when I try new things, the fears around my body and impostor syndrome as people started calling me inspirational even though I see myself as an average climber... something I still struggle with today. I also blogged about what climbing has given me.

Climbing has given me so much. Through climbing, I have found friends, a lifestyle, my life's purpose. When I'm stressed, the wall is my outlet. When I need support, the wall is there for me. The wall has become a mirror of my life. When I'm scared, fatigued or frustrated, it shows in my climbing. Climbing is also the only sport I have found that doesn't dislocate my joints. In fact, it helps me realign my joints and reduce my pain levels. The strength gains I have made through climbing have improved my general quality of life too. I can do more at home without running out of energy on my good days.

In the three years that I've been climbing, I've been diagnosed with Ehlers-Danlos syndrome, lymphoedema in my left arm, polycystic ovaries, inflammatory bowel disease (suspected Crohn's disease) and orthostatic intolerance (suspected postural orthostatic tachycardia syndrome). I'm still being investigated for other complications as my health continues to deteriorate.

I have become an ambassador for LimbPower, the leading amputee charity for getting amputees and limb-different people into sport, as well as for Ehlers-Danlos Support UK, and a patron for Grit&Rock, a foundation supporting girls from deprived backgrounds to reach their life potential through climbing.

One of the things that struck me as a paraclimber was the fact that I only met other paras in competition. Unlike other groups, paraclimbers didn't really have opportunities to meet socially and climb, so we didn't. As with my cancer experience, the paraclimbing experience was a bit isolating. It's great to climb with able-bodied climbers, but I felt the lack of a community of paras. With my public profile growing, paraclimbers in London would get in touch with me, and we would all lament the fact that we didn't really have a social safe space to cater to our needs. While we understand why people call us inspirational, it's nice being in a space when you know you're not different to anyone else. It's nice knowing we can sit back and say we really are having a crap day and it won't be questioned, even if we "look well".

This was when the idea of Paraclimbing London came about. A space where people with visible and invisible disabilities, including mental health issues and cancer, can come together and climb, whether you are already a climber or not. Together, my friend Anna Knight and I created Paraclimbing London, and within a year we had 200 members. We also try to address some of the safety and awareness issues that surround disability generally and specifically disability in climbing. How do we make sure our visually impaired climbers don't fall on someone who walks under them on the bouldering mat? How do we find ways for our neurodivergent climbers to enjoy the sport while not feeling overwhelmed?

Life today is a constant challenge. I juggle a hugely variable health picture and a crazy number of symptoms that can make or break my day or even my hour. I work nearly full-time, train hard when I can and support the charities I work with in any way I can, while also writing about issues that we as a society are pretty bad at talking about. This includes delving pretty deeply into my own feelings and being openly vulnerable about them. Showing society it's OK to talk about the things we are not great at talking about means talking about it in the first place. I talk openly about the days that frustrate me to the point of crying or the days when I can't get out of bed because I'm too dizzy. My coaches both watch my body signals carefully because they know I still want to train even when I shouldn't (though I'm not particularly good at hiding how bad things can get).

I've been learning how to cope with my bad days. Accepting that it's OK to not be OK, be that physically or mentally, but that it's so important to keep striving for progress.

I balance my life between taking self-care hours or days and pushing myself out of my comfort zone.

Sometimes I have days when I despair, that *why me?* day when even a sock on the floor will have me upset (I live a rather cluttered life, so there's always stuff on the floor!). Getting out of the house on those days feels like an emotionally impossible task. Eating chicken wings and ice cream or curling up in bed with my Simba toy are my solutions, as well as, again, accepting that sometimes life really does just suck. Having an outlet also helps. For me, it's talking or writing. I post a blog or chat to my friends.

My toughest challenge has been learning to pace myself on my good days so that I can have more good days. When healthy people push their limits, they normally recover and are OK to push again a couple of days later. When people with chronic illness push hard? It can backfire badly. It's such a delicate balance trying to train hard while not pushing myself to the point of breaking down.

There are days when I wake up feeling fantastic and then I'm using my desk at work to support myself a few hours later because things have degraded quickly. There are days where I've prepped all my meals but my gut flares up and I'm restricted to liquid foods until things settle. It's exhausting, frustrating, upsetting and I do really allow myself to feel all of that so I can release it and stop holding the baggage. After that, I always try and find something to celebrate, identify something I learned and set my intention for the next day because tomorrow is always a new day.

On my utterly awful days, I'm grateful for being alive and really basic things like breathing or taking a few steps. It's on those days where I have had to learn to accept that walking to the kitchen is a triumph. It's those days that make me appreciate the little things and help me become more resilient.

On awesome days, I'll celebrate multiple personal bests, I'll be grateful for a functional body and I'll be recognizing that these days are few and far between. I breathe the moment in, imprint the amazing feelings, imbibe them into my body so that I can remind myself of what this feels like on my next run of bad days.

ALONE IN THE JUNGLE:

RIDING THE REAL HO CHI MINH TRAIL

ANTONIA BOLINGBROKE-KENT

Antonia Bolingbroke-Kent is a travel writer and broadcaster with a particular love of wandering alone through remote regions. The author of three books, she's raised more than £60,000 for charitable causes and once held the highly competitive Guinness World Record for the longest ever journey by autorickshaw.

Antonia's love of extreme solo travel has seen her trek across the Eastern Himalayas in search of Shangri-La, follow the remains of the Ho Chi Minh Trail on a small pink motorcycle and interview Naga rebel commanders high in the mountains of the Indo-Myanmar border.

Her latest book, *Land of the Dawn-lit Mountains: A Journey across Arunachal Pradesh – India's Forgotten Frontier* (Simon & Schuster, 2017), was shortlisted for the 2018 Stanford Adventure Travel Book of the Year.

Antonia writes for *The Telegraph*, the *Financial Times*, *Wanderlust*, *The Guardian* and BBC Radio 4's *From Our Own Correspondent*. Her first radio documentary was aired on Radio 4 in early 2020. In 2019 she was the recipient of the Royal Geographical Society's prestigious Neville Shulman Challenge Award. A regular public speaker, Antonia has entertained audiences at the Royal Geographical Society, the *FT Weekend* Festival, Kendal Mountain Festival, Cheltenham Festival and more.

Find out more about Antonia at:

W: www.theitinerant.co.uk

T: @AntsBK

I: @antsbk

Fuelled by fear and pounded by rain, I squelched and slipped through the deserted forest. For the first time in my life death felt a possibility; a stupid, pointless, lonely end on the aptly named Mondulkiri Death Highway. I cursed myself for being so stubborn and stupid, for ignoring the warnings, for being so obsessive about following the Ho Chi Minh Trail. If I died, it would be death by hubris, my own stupid fault. My only hope was to keep walking. But for how long, I could only guess.

———

Five weeks earlier I'd wobbled through the Hanoi traffic, my pink Honda Cub a mere dot in the barging torrent of man and machine. For the next six weeks I'd be following the Ho Chi Minh Trail, a legendary transport network which had once spread 12,000 miles through Vietnam, Laos and Cambodia. The means by which Uncle Ho's communist North were able to send men and supplies to defeat the American-backed South, the trail had been the fulcrum of the Vietnam War. I'd first encountered the trail while working on a BBC documentary the previous year and was soon hooked: before the shoot was over I'd decided to come back, alone, to explore what remained of this once mighty web – before time, nature and development swallowed it forever.

Aided by *Top Gear*'s 2008 Vietnam Special, biking has surged in popularity in Vietnam. But while in 2013 scores of travellers rode a tourist-friendly, tarmac version of the trail between Hanoi and Ho Chi Minh City, only a handful followed its gnarly guts over the Truong Son mountains into Laos. Even fewer traced it south into the wild eastern reaches of Cambodia. I wanted to do both. Unlike the hundreds of thousands of North Vietnamese who walked, drove and worked on the trail in the sixties and seventies, I wouldn't have to deal with a daily deluge of bombs. But UXO, unexploded ordnance, littered my route south and cerebral malaria, dengue fever and dysentery were still prevalent. Whatever happened, it wasn't going to be an easy ride.

Despite these dangers, I was intent on riding alone, on stripping away the protective blanket of companionship and seeing what I was really made of. How would I react when my bike ground to a halt in the middle of a river? Could I hack days and nights alone in the jungle? Only through the purity of solitude would I find the answers.

From the outset, I knew I wanted to ride a Honda Cub. With three gears, slender city wheels and brakes that would barely stop a bolting snail, the Honda Cub isn't the most obvious off-roader. But with my meagre budget and limited mechanical know-how, the cheap, idiot-proof bike suited me perfectly. Sourced and pimped for me by friends in Hanoi, my 25-year-old 85cc model cost a mere £300.

Vietnam was trail-lite, a gentle introduction to what lay ahead. My bike – which I'd christened the Pink Panther – spun along the smooth tarmac of the Ho Chi Minh Highway, and roadside cafes, fuel and cheap hotels were in abundance. In a nation of 90 million people, I was rarely alone. Everywhere

I stopped, curious crowds gathered around me, firing me with friendly questions. Where was I from? Where was I going? Where was my husband? Why was I alone? Never has a phrase book been so thoroughly thumbed.

At times the Vietnamese were a little *too* friendly. Twice in the first week, as I sat slurping noodle soup at a roadside shack, men approached and offered me 500,000 dong, about £15, for a lunchtime quickie. I wasn't sure if it was the pink bike, the fact that I was a lone Western female or the irresistible cocktail of the two. Sweaty, devoid of make-up and dressed in biker gear, I couldn't see the appeal.

Aside from a few dull, misty days south of Hanoi, the scenery was fantastic, alternating between cascading rice paddies, sugar cane fields and patches of verdant forest. Dawdling along at 20 miles per hour, I drank in this Otherness: men in pith helmets – a hangover from years of war – led sullen water buffaloes along the verge; scores of ancient Honda Cubs chuntered along, obscured under titanic loads; farmers tended to their paddies, hinged at the waist like compasses; and everywhere men and women chopped and loaded newly harvested sugar cane, piling it on to waiting buffalo carts. It wasn't long before my initial nerves dissipated, replaced by the soaring elation one only gets from the open road. Already I didn't want this journey to end.

After a week I reached the Mu Gia Pass, a narrow conduit through the wall of the Truong Son mountains that had served as North Vietnam's principal route to the trail in Laos. Blasted by US bombs and defoliants, nowadays the 418-metre pass is a quiet border crossing little used by Westerners. I'd been warned that I'd never make it across, that the Lao border guards were known for turning back foreigners, that I'd have to make a lengthy diversion to a more tourist-friendly crossing. But I was determined to try.

Miraculously, I made it through the border and was soon standing on the other side of the pass admiring the new world before me. And what a new world it was: as if the mountains were the heavy velvet curtain of a theatre, drawn back to reveal a wholly different reality. Only 6 hours earlier, I had ridden through a drizzly Vietnamese dawn, my fleece and motorbike jacket zipped up against the cold. Now I stood in a thin cotton shirt, pounded by 40-degree heat, the empty, karst-rimmed valley below me shimmering in the noon inferno. Laos, the hot, sparsely populated crucible of the trail, was going to be very different.

The following morning I rode south through a Lost World landscape of tinder-dry jungle and pinnacles of slate-grey karst. Panther's tyres, which I'd let down a few bars to help with the dirt, crunched over red laterite, sending clouds of dust billowing about me. Formerly a main north–south artery of the trail, the roadside was punctured with bomb craters, a reminder of America's extreme efforts to destroy the trail. Between 1965 and 1973 over two million tonnes of ordnance were dropped on this neutral country, an onslaught which gave Laos the deadly accolade of being the most bombed country per capita on earth, a title it retains to this day.

Many of these bombs still remain, a fact I was reminded of that afternoon when foolishly walking through the scrub in search of an old Vietnamese anti-aircraft gun emplacement. In a pile of leaves inches from the path lay a single cluster bomb submunition. One wrong step and this tennis-ball-sized killer would have blown me to bits.

I rode south through thick jungle and scruffy tribal villages, scattering oinking black piglets and scrawny chickens as

I passed. Foreigners rarely, if ever, came this way and while some of the ragged children ran excitedly after me, others simply froze and stared open-mouthed. Several groups of women hitched up their sarongs and bolted into the forest, terrified, like deer startled by a wolf. Nowhere else in the world has this ever happened to me. It was most odd.

Everywhere there were reminders of the war. Stilted huts were built on cluster-bomb casings, boys paddled in canoes made from discarded aeroplane fuel canisters and cows wore bells fashioned from old mortar fuses. In one village, Ban Phanop, the wing of a crashed US F-4 fighter leaned against a tree and two live 500-pound bombs lay under a family's hut, waiting to be sold for scrap metal. Further south, around the old trail command post at La Hap, I rode down a dark, eerie track flanked by bomb craters and the rusted remains of North Vietnamese trucks.

In this remote, inaccessible region accommodation options were limited. I spent most nights in government-run guesthouses-cum-brothels – grim establishments seeping with leprous patches of damp. Food was equally basic: I subsisted on a diet of sticky rice, eggs, warm Coca-Cola, Beerlao and gritty Vietnamese coffee laced with dollops of condensed milk.

But I hadn't come for Egyptian cotton and fine cuisine, and the tough, exhilarating riding more than made up for it. One day I'd be sliding down sun-dappled jungle tracks, my wheels spinning through lakes of orange mud; the next I'd be struggling up steep ladders of basalt, yelping like a Soviet weightlifter as I heaved and paddled the bike upward. I bumped over original trail cobblestones, sliced through deep white sand, buzzed across parched grass plateaux dotted with pines and spun along dirt tracks in obliterating veils of dust. By the time

I reached each grotty guesthouse I was caked in a carapace of mud and dust, drenched in sweat, famished and in dire need of a Beerlao. I wouldn't have wanted to be anywhere else.

Rivers were my other obstacle. Generally it was a case of throttle-on-feet-up-and-ride, hoping the engine wouldn't conk out or I'd get an ignominious ducking. Other crossings were more perilous, such as having to balance on a terrifyingly narrow, wobbly canoe as a toothless old man pushed me across with a single pole. On one occasion Panther was carried across by a gaggle of glistening, nut-brown children.

Panther was less delighted with the task at hand. A few weeks into the journey, she began to sound like a bronchitic tractor and one day, in a half-a-horse village in Laos, she refused to start at all. A scrawny, chain-smoking local mechanic quickly diagnosed the problem: the cam chain and sprockets had gone, in turn damaging the valves and cylinder barrel. The next day, after a £35 engine rebuild, we were back in action. But by the time I reached Cambodia the incident had been repeated twice. It was hard to fathom why the same thing kept happening over and over again. It could have been due to poor quality parts, or each mechanic setting the cam timing wrong. Or maybe it was simply that my "indestructible" Cub couldn't cope with the Ho Chi Minh Trail.

The next border was quick and easy, and soon I was riding south across the heat-scorched Mekong lowlands of Cambodia. On either side was the same red earth and stilted houses as Laos; only the billboards advertizing Khmer beers and the upcoming elections spoke of a new country. It's funny how we always want what we don't have. There were times in Laos when I would have given my last dime for a sliver of tarmac. But in the next few days, as I buzzed along new Chinese-built highways through miles and miles of rubber plantations, I craved the mountains and jungle I'd left behind.

I also missed the trail. From scant references in books and a few clues on my old Vietnamese trail map I knew it had fingered its way through the jungles of north-east Cambodia. But time, civil war and the genocidal Khmer Rouge had largely wiped it from existence and memory, and clues were thin on the ground. Even hiring a grumpy translator for a few days threw little light on the matter. Riding east through rubber plantations and illegally logged jungle, we asked numerous village elders if they knew anything of the trail. Myopic Jarai chiefs, whose huts were perched between multiple bomb craters, shook their heads. A skeletal old man living in Bâ Kham, a crater-pocked village marked as a supply base on the old map, eyed me suspiciously and denied all knowledge. Even if they could remember, I realized they weren't going to tell me. Persecuted by Pol Pot and looked down upon by the lowland Khmers, the north-east's tribal minorities had rarely come off well from contact with questioning outsiders.

South of here lay the Mondulkiri Death Highway, a 90-mile dirt track through uninhabited forest soon to be upgraded by the Chinese. The *Lonely Planet* warned it should only be attempted in dry season by "hardcore bikers" with "years of experience and an iron backside". However, since the only other way south was a 300-mile diversion back via the Mekong, it didn't occur to me not to attempt it. Panther and I had survived Laos – there was nothing we couldn't tackle now.

But early rains had churned the track into a morass of lakes, ruts and bogs through which I splashed, struggled and heaved, my legs swallowed by the sticky slime. Stubbornly I persisted. Although I was only averaging a few miles an hour, if I kept buggering on – metre by metre, minute by minute – I'd make it to the next village before nightfall. Even when the only human I saw – a young man with two dead cockerels strung over his moped's handlebars – stopped and motioned for me not to go on, I ignored his advice and ploughed on anyway. *If you listened to everyone in life who told you not to go on, you would never get anywhere*, I thought. Even if he was right, I had to see for myself.

As dusk fell, Panther sunk in the mire for the umpteenth time that day – but now not even the brute force of fear could move her. Suddenly the situation was critical. Without help it was impossible for me to haul her out. But I was alone in the jungle and very low on water. I had no choice but to leave her and walk for help.

Twilight melted into darkness as I trudged north, the air alive with an eerie, echoing orchestra of frogs; their croaks, trills and gribbits bounced off the trees in stereo sound. A lone parrot flapped over my head, its silhouette imprinted in the twilight. Plodding through the rain, I talked to myself to keep calm, acutely aware that situations like this can go very wrong very quickly. I was alone. I was a long way from help. I was weak and dizzy from hunger, physical exertion and dehydration. I only had a few sips of water left. I'd been exposed to extreme heat all day and had lost a lot of liquid through sweat. I was beginning to feel disorientated, convinced I could hear a digger nearby. Sometimes it was ahead of me, sometimes behind, sometimes somewhere in the trees. But in reality it was nowhere.

If it hadn't been for a Cambodian road workers' camp I stumbled into hours later, dangerously dehydrated and partially delirious, things could have been very different. I'll never forget those kind men who took me in, fed me rice and water and helped me retrieve the bike the following morning. She was no longer starting, so I got her trucked the 30 miles to Ban Lung, the nearest town, where she had her *fourth* engine rebuild.

The young Vietnamese guards stamped me back into their country. Ho Chi Minh City was only 150 miles south. So near the end, my emotions returned to the see-sawing unpredictability of the first few days of my journey. Weeks of hard riding, extreme heat, poor diet and lack of sleep were chipping away at my energy levels and I knew it was time to finish. But following the trail had been thrilling, engrossing, poignant and ceaselessly compelling. I didn't want it to end.

Bubbling with nerves and excitement, I buzzed toward Ho Chi Minh City through a panorama of mirror-flat paddies and drooping palms. Teenage girls bicycled in giggling groups, wooden carts pulled by handsome conker-brown oxen trundled along the verge and swarms of mopeds carried families, trussed-up pigs and cages of cowering dogs. Through the middle lurched overcrowded buses and hooting trucks, neither of which slowed for anything or anyone. I crawled along, watching the road and my mirrors obsessively, keen to avoid a last-minute accident.

Gradually the buildings became taller, the palms disappeared and the traffic swelled to a raging flood. Everywhere there was traffic, mopeds, engine noise and masked faces under multicoloured helmets. I was in Ho Chi Minh. At last, the Reunification Palace, my final destination, loomed ahead.

"We've made it, Panther," I said out loud, as my wheels touched the gates. "We've bloody made it."

A group of Japanese tourists stopped photographing the palace and looked at me.

I couldn't believe we'd actually done it. For 10 minutes I just sat there, staring at the white facade, smiling, savouring the moment. Six weeks, three countries, 2,000 miles, four engine rebuilds and one hell of an adventure later, my Ho Chi Mission was finally over.

PSIREN SONG

BETH FRENCH

From wheelchair bound to world-class athlete, **Beth French** relishes stretching the horizons of her own possibilities, tackling seemingly impossible feats of endurance and adventure.

Beth suffered with ME, myalgic encephalomyelitis, from the age of 10, and by 17 she was in a wheelchair. Overcoming debilitation, she forged a path to ultimate health her own way and studied indigenous healthcare practices from around the world – from lomi lomi in Hawaii to spending time ordained as a nun in a Buddhist monastery.

Beth is the first woman to swim the notorious Ka'iwi (the Channel of Bones, in Hawaii) twice, and the first person ever to swim from Cornwall to the Isles of Scilly. In 2017 she was named as one of the World Open Water Swimming Association's 50 most adventurous open water women and is proud to be an ambassador for the First Women UK project. She is the subject of the documentary *Against the Tides* by BAFTA-nominated director Stefan Stuckert.

With all her exploring, she still maintains she is ordinary and that adventure is in all of us, every day. Beth lives in Somerset with her autistic son, Dylan, who is her inspiration, constant adventure companion and chief egger-onner.

Find out more about Beth at:
W: bethfrench.co.uk
I: @bethfrenchlives
F: @bethfrenchlives

The psiren song of adventure has as many voices as there are people to hear them. They draw us ever onward to seek out the unfound, to reach the peaks and depths, to search deep within ourselves for the very heart of what it means to quest. She is a tough mistress, but a generous one. Whether those in her thrall are traversing hills and vales, snowy mountains or arid deserts, they are enraptured with curiosity unbound and infectious intent.

For me, it is the ocean. Untainted by barriers and assistance, I like to head for the horizon, immersed in the ultimate crucible, the sensory overload and deprivation combined. For me, channel swimming is a by-product of a lifelong urge to be in the sea. And the "rules" are that I must start on dry land, enter the water with no insulation, flotation or propulsion assistance of any kind and keep going under my own steam until I reach the other side. No rest, no respite, no way out. Inter-island, inter-country and inter-continent – I have been drawn to them all.

It is a relentless pursuit – you are face down in the water hour after hour. The only human "contact" is every hour when my trusty support crew accompanying me by boat drop me a bottle of premixed carbohydrate and electrolyte fluid. Like a sea otter, I drink on my back, for 30–40 seconds, then flip back over and I'm gone again. My adventuring cannot happen without a trusted team for support, but it is so very much an internal, personal experience. You are on your own out there, in your head.

The sea has long been used in literature and art to signify our emotions, our subconscious. It has come to embody our deepest fears and our need for adventure. On the one hand, the ebb and flow, the rise and fall, is soporific, and most people's imaginations go to relaxation imagery... but it is also the murky depths, the fathomless and endless ocean. The edge of the map, unknown territory. Here be monsters. We know more of the surface of the moon than we do about the bottom of the sea.

It is here I can pour myself – mind and body, all that I have worked for and all that I am. To test my mettle and weigh my worth my own way. It also scratches a most intimate itch – vulnerability. The fear of it and the need for it are equal in my mind, and channel swimming is a forum wherein I can challenge myself to the point of complete vulnerability. I peel away my layers and use everything I have and then some, all while I entrust my existence to someone else – the support crew, who know me, but also the pilot, who I may never have met before. I lay bare my hopes and dreams, my strengths, demons and weaknesses for all to see.

Expose my soul while someone watches my back and lets me go through my own personal hell and back without being able to assist – and share the heaven that is sunrise over the ocean, or phosphorescence spiralling off my fingertips.

———

I cannot remember a time I did not dream of swimming straight out from shore – when I was a small child, my parents were told: "She'll join the merchant navy, that one." But I was confused. I didn't want to be on a boat. I wanted my whole body in the water. I wanted to self-propel myself someplace else. But to swim the English Channel – to swim from here to a whole other country – that was a grand adventure. I was merely a third child – third daughter, no less – of a farmer in Somerset. No sporting background, no contacts, not wealthy and not remotely able to see a way to actualize my dream. And grand adventures were for a different breed, were they not? The rich, or the born and bred families with African siroccos in their hair, or Arctic gazes instilled at birth. Olympic athletes gone rogue.

And so I dreamed.

But even though I was an active child, a tomboy, climbing trees and being as feral as I was able, my life changed at a precious age. At ten, I awoke unable to raise myself from the bed. It felt like liquid lead was coursing through my veins. My brain was full of fog and I was scared. And just like that, suddenly and arbitrarily, my body was not the one I knew only yesterday – my mind was addled and I was thrown into tumult, terrified at being isolated and unrecognizable even to my family and friends, let alone myself. For years I lived a half-life, trapped in my body, unable to understand or express how it felt to be cast adrift and locked in all at once. I fought my body and mind – struggled to maintain normality in a radically inconsistent self. Random and sporadic, my health would surge and I would burst forward, eager to achieve and gain a foothold in the bright and promising future the adults in my life swore was mine if only I could stay the course... and then crash.

After seven long years of self-doubt, self-harm and increasingly severe peaks and troughs, I succumbed completely to a wheelchair. I was finally diagnosed with ME, myalgic encephalomyelitis. While it came as a relief that there was a name to this malady, it was devastating because the prognosis was that I might live my entire life like this. Fits and starts, unable to string a coherent life together. And purpose burned within me – the need to catch up on lost time, the rage of years I felt were wasted and all the pain of being left behind while my peers grew up and away while I felt hemmed in and stuck. At the deepest I fell, bedridden and barely conscious for weeks on end, all I had were dreams. They pained me, felt like cruel visions of the never-never, empty hopes, but as I pondered and willed, a few ideas kept repeating themselves until they crystallized into hardened nuggets of yearning.

I can't tell you how I got better, only that it was a long and circuitous road full of ups and downs and many wrong turns. But I started to see a clear way forward. And with all the pushing I had had to do for over a decade, I found that with energy my single-pointed drive could be turned outward rather than in on myself. And as my twenties passed in a blur of travel, I discovered that the relationship I never developed with my body – that most take for granted – could be forged in the very place I turned to for solace. Even on my darkest day, I could float and find peace. A bath, a stream, a lake, but more than anything, the sea. I found myself there. Found a way back to my body. Not for me the easy taking for granted that most people enjoy. Mine is a tenuous, fragile nod at a shy, wild creature, skittish and flighty. But in the sea, we meet and play.

It was in Hawaii that I fell in love. Spinning and spiralling, diving and dancing. My whole being was a sense organ –

feeling the water move around me, move me. I started to marvel at the wonder of feeling, the first unfurling tendrils of trust peeking out and brushing alongside this new-found joy at what my body can do. Water so clear I could track my path across a bay by following the impressions in the sand of the movement of the water, mesmerized by the starburst of light as the sun shone down through the water below me. Entranced, finally, with being in love with my body for what it can do.

And so I lived to swim. I fed my body, nurtured it – listened intently to its needs – in order that I could spend time with it, in it, in the sea. I learned about health, I studied all manner of approaches to natural well-being, all to bring me more time and space in this brave new world I had found. And the longer I was in the water, the more I settled into myself. The more my mind cleared and all else fell away. On dry land, if I didn't get in the sea for days, I became a shaky faun, stumbling once again with self-doubt – others' expectations overriding my delicate sense of self. And so I would run back to the sea. I spent more and more time in its embrace, finding more and more reasons to carve this time out as important. Because on dry land I felt all at sea.

Those precious years have left an indelible scar and one I wear proudly. When I turned 30, and found myself in another brave new world – of single parenthood and feeling more than a little shaky – I looked back at the times I had trusted myself, when I had felt most strong and fulfilled. I wanted my son to have that version of me as his mother. I wanted to share with him those qualities that had led me to swim with wild dolphins, to hear whale song so loud it made me vibrate and feel like I was melting; to understand the belief in oneself that time in deep meditation awoke. So I looked back at those embryonic ideas I had trapped in my own mind as a bedridden teen. And I realized I had inadvertently struck off dream after dream... all bar the one that had been there the longest – the one I feared the most as out of my reach – to swim to France.

And so I chose a different path to the one expected. Without family support, as a self-employed mother, I set about proving to myself that I needn't drown on dry land. I needn't get washed away in life's rip tide. I could navigate these waters and chart my own course. I needed to prove my trust in my body was well placed. So I trained while Dylan (man of the ocean) was asleep, I carried him hiking and towed him in a dinghy in the sea. I found purpose in adventure and in adventure I found my answers.

Two years later, having put Dylan to bed in a caravan on the outskirts of Dover, with a childminder, I was standing on Shakespeare Beach at 2.30 a.m. in nothing but a swimming costume, a swimming cap and a pair of goggles, covered from head to foot in Vaseline and feeling like I had already won. I had made it to the start. I was ready to swim to France. A lifetime of dreaming and I had made it. Whatever happened, I had made it here.

It was pitch black, with no stars or moon above. The support boat was nothing but a collection of distant lights and it was impossible to judge distance. But the shush of the water at my feet, the inky, silky blackness was calling me onward. The lull of the memory of all the peace I have ever found in the water walked into the Channel with me and I smiled as I stroked away from the shore, from "home", from everything I knew. I know the normal response to standing in the dark, facing 40 kilometres of dark, frigid (barely 16°C), ferry-laden, jellyfish-strewn water wearing precious little is to back away and find a nice, warm, solid room with lights and laughter, but I felt free. I felt liberated and so very, very grateful.

That first channel swim contained every lesson I have learned since – I was merely unaware of them at the time. I was so overcome with sheer joy at the very notion that I was actually here, doing it, that I missed out on a lot of the trials, tribulations and mental tumult I was expecting. For me, the tough parts were done. The challenge to stand in the face of expectation, to choose different and to doggedly self-believe – against family, personal history and societal norm. To train, as a young first-time mum, to find space and time amid growing concerns over my son's development... to listen to my inner voice telling me that even so, with all these stacked up, mine is still just as right a path as that predicated by others.

So, the first 10 hours of swimming to France were nothing but pure pleasure. I remember switching my breathing pattern to look only to the left as the sky lightened, colour leached back into the world and a peerless sunrise seared itself into my lifelong memory as an overriding feature of that adventure. I remember being delightfully bemused at the soft, silky aqua of the water mid-Channel – not the chewy brown sludge of my imagination! I vividly remember the moment when I noticed the tankers were indeed now going the other way. Near the French coast the north-east Channel acts as a one-way system – then you cross the separation zone, which is a no man's land to keep the shipping apart. So, noting the megaliths travelling in the opposite direction tells a swimmer they are swimming into the south-west lane – the one-way system on the French side – and that they are two thirds of the way to France.

I remember being told that I was only one and a half hours from landing and about to hit a band of current that often ends people's hopes of reaching France. After 10 hours of swimming, I would now have to sprint for up to an hour. My arms were like limp, overcooked spaghetti. Every emotion was spent. I was in a state of grace, but I wasn't aware of a tank to have anything left in. And yet I could see cars on the shore. I could make out individual windows in French houses. The water was warming; the sun was still high in a stunning blue sky. I was swimming to France. And I was enjoying it. So I got my head down with my proverbial chin up and threw my arms round in a windmill, urging my tired legs to assist, my aching lungs to work more efficiently, to pass as much oxygen to my lagging muscles as they could.

And then BANG, BANG, BANG went the captain's arm on the side of the boat.

Confused and disconcerted, I lifted my head.

"Forget the landing – tide's turned, tide's turned."

I looked up to where only 10 minutes before there had been tangible land – only to see a completely different view. Gone was the rocky Cap Gris-Nez we were aiming for, and instead there opened up a huge deep bay stretching into the distance.

It is hard to describe the process I went through in the moments when I realized that the surety of landing soon was gone – the digging deep to find power and speed after 10 hours of swimming was wasted, futile; the rug had been well and truly pulled rudely from under me. The endgame just changed the rules. They say channel swimming is 80 per cent mental (largely because you have to be 80 per cent mental to get in the water...) because you will get tired, you will hurt, you will doubt. The ocean is alive and fickle so there is no certainty, even when you are within a stone's throw of completing your plan your way. You are at the beck and call of Mother Nature in the most visceral way, totally immersed, at her mercy. I huffed my exasperation.

The skipper simply said, "Aim for that speck of a cluster of white buildings waaaay across the bay. Could be three hours, could be another eight... The ladder of the boat is five metres. France is over there. Which do you want more – to stop swimming or to get to France?"

This was the cruel truth of channel swimming laid bare. With the current already galloping, the tide had now joined it, and where on the coast I could finally make landfall was anybody's guess. To be already exhausted and still with no discernible end in reach, I was reminded of hearing of this moment. *Now is when the real Channel swim begins*, I thought. Make or break time. I had also heard horror tales of Channel swims ending less than 100 metres from shore due to poor visibility, so I knew to thank my lucky stars that it was "only" time and distance that were between me and the shore. There was not a moment's indecision. I wasn't broken, I had had my expectations dislocated.

And that was when I learned the most valuable lesson that has come back again and again until I recognized it for what it was. I went through all the tricks of psychology to find energy. Swim for your supporters – confusing as too emotional... Swim for the naysayers – dig deep and prove them wrong. Eugh, not my bag... Get aggressive and grind it out – yuck! The opposite of why I get in the water... Swim for my son – tempting, but he was proud of me yesterday, and he'll be proud of me no matter what. I'd rather teach him that it's better to have tried and not got there than not try – or kick yourself and label it failure if you don't get where you thought you were going.

So I looked at it from afar... I was possibly a little detached from reality anyway by this point. Why was I here? Because swimming is where I find myself – it's where I can put all the pressures I feel on dry land down and just be happy in my body. So I learned to apply a different kind of strength to the one I had relied on so often. I had only valued the strength of never, ever stopping. Of never giving up: the kind of strength that is often mislabelled and often wrongly (in my opinion) synonymous with success. It is what we are sold and is often the only kind of strength we are told is good. In the water that day, I learned the value of the strength to let go. Let go of the fear, let go of the fatigue, let go of the need to please others and achieve. This was my personal time to shine. Not for others, but for myself. And in that moment, I became my own hero. My best friend, my advocate. I stopped suffering. Pain was just my body's way of telling me to adjust my stroke to be more efficient. I granted myself the time and space to enjoy the rest of my swim to France.

And my proudest moment was not staggering up on to a small French beach with people coming off the sea wall to congratulate me – epic though it was. It happened about an hour before my foot touched dry land. I was again within spitting distance. The bay was shallow and I could see the bottom. I could see the promenaders out in the late afternoon sunshine and I lifted my head and asked the time. Normally, I don't want to know – time is so flexible and can be cruel – but this was with a purpose. I demanded to be told – and, while looking at the French shore, I was given my best moment ever. When they told me the time – about 4.30 p.m. – I realized that

I could swim to France and be back in England in time to put my son to bed. I could complete my mission to put motherhood first! And it was like a huge oxygen bubble burst through me. I was smiling, giggling (possibly slightly delusional by now), and I was doing it my way.

Standing on the French shore, this new-found confidence coursing through my veins, I no longer feared making different, often tough choices. My future was in my hands. I accepted the reins with anticipation rather than anxiety. I am so fortunate to have swum such incredible swims. I have seen awe-inspiring things and confronted most people's worst nightmare – encountering a 7-foot tiger shark 20 miles out to sea in the pitch dark with nothing but a kayak alongside me – and I keep coming back to what kept me going on that first Channel crossing. A goal is a destination – somewhere to aim. Passion and drive get you going. But when the chips are down, it is letting go of what's holding you back that allows you to keep going. Even when the destination is the very thing you end up letting go of. There is no failure once you've started. The learning along the way, the chance and ability to try, is the very essence of adventure itself. Whatever happens on the road, trail, path you're on is an adventure. It's a way of looking at what's ahead of you.

KAYAK-TIVISM:
PADDLING
THE BALKANS
WITH PURPOSE

CARMEN KUNTZ

Carmen Kuntz grew up canoeing on the lakes and rivers of northern Canada and became a freelance writer after finishing a geography degree and a raft-guiding career near Ottawa. She writes for outdoor adventure sports publications worldwide while managing the river conservation NGO Balkan River Defence with her partner from the banks of Slovenia's Soča River. White water is the most consistent element in her life and a paddle is her favourite tool.

Find out more about Carmen at:
W: carmenekuntz.com
I: @carmenekuntz

Sitting cross-legged in the dust, I adjust my position on the cold ground, exhaling into my cupped palms before stuffing them into my pockets. The mid-September air is damp and cold in the Valbona River valley in northern Albania. I'm fidgeting in part to keep warm, but also to release nervous energy. I am part of a chain of 25 people – white-water kayakers and local villagers – sitting in the dirt so close together our shoulders touch and folded legs overlap. We have created a blockade, a human wall to obstruct access to the construction site of an illegal hydropower dam on the Valbona River. A dam here would kill the river, and with it, the traditional way of living as well as the endemic flora and fauna, which all depend on the river for life. If workers and machines can't get to the river, then its churning rapids, carved limestone canyons, polished-pebble riverbed and crystal clear, turquoise waters – which we were skimming across in our kayaks the day before – are safe. For the moment at least. That is why we are here. Kayakers turned activists who refuse to let greed destroy the last wild rivers of the Balkans.

The stars were still bright in the sky when we crawled out of warm sleeping bags an hour ago, piled into vans and arrived at the riverside construction site. In a blur of head torches, handshakes and hugs, we were greeted by locals – fellow river defenders and the real heroes of this story. We hung up banners with strong messages like *Mos ma prek Valbonën* (*Hands off the Valbona*). GoPros – previously attached to kayaking helmets – were attached to nearby trees, repurposed as hidden surveillance cameras. Then, we sat down. There will be no movement from our group of international white-water kayakers. Just peaceful resistance that the river conservation movement Balkan River Defence (BRD) is known for. We are protesting to protect a river we play on, and more importantly, a river that locals and wildlife depend on.

As daylight arrives, the excitement of rebellion mixes with fear and anticipation. We are far from home and for many kayakers, this is their first environmental protest – their first real act of defiance. Pair that with the political environment of corruption and violence in Albania, and this morning is more adrenaline-packed than yesterday's paddle down the tight and technical white water of the Valbona River. Everyone is silent, preparing for a long day of direct action in this remote valley of the Balkans.

———

The Balkan Peninsula extends out of south-eastern Europe into the Adriatic Sea. From Slovenia to Greece, the Balkans cover over 470,000 km², roughly twice the size of the UK. The geopolitical history here is complicated, but the topographic story is simple. On a map, the Balkans are comprised of a thick web of blue lines illustrating the area's rich river systems. European environmental conservation groups call the Balkans 'the blue heart of Europe', referring to clear creeks, steep canyons, stunning waterfalls and lush forests that make it the most pristine freshwater network in Europe. This is one of the last places where the snow melts in the mountains and flows undisturbed to the sea. But the hydropower dam craze that is sweeping the region is changing that.

The story of the Valbona River is repeated all over the Balkans. Largely fuelled by foreign investment saturated in corruption, small dams in the Balkans provide an outlet for money laundering while disregarding environmental compliance and policy. The energy these dams create is not delivered to local populations but instead exported, while private hydropower plant owners fill their pockets with the EU subsidies granted for "green" energy suppliers. Sitting beside me is 23-year-old Liridon Mustafaj, a Valbona local who explains to me how the construction company building this dam forged the signatures of locals, even using fake signatures of deceased residents to push forward construction. Greed is strong, but locals who unite and passionate resistance can be stronger. Liridon has never been in a kayak and has never seen the jaw-dropping curves and cambers that decades of water movement have carved into this incredible canyon. He has never seen the calm pools inside smooth vaulted grottos that this dam will destroy. Yet he explains to us how he grew up with the river and describes the Valbona as a member of his family.

Kayaks give us an opportunity to get to know rivers like the Valbona through exploration and play. They also allow us to see stretches of river seldom seen by humans and likely never seen by locals: canyons and rapids that evoke respect and even fear from locals, who are unable to navigate technical rapids and tight canyons and thus have only one perspective of the river – from the bank looking down.

The day before, in between meetings with locals to organize the road blockade, we scrambled down the steep bank from the riverside road that dead ends in the Valbona valley, snapped spray skirts on cockpit rims and pushed off the rocky shore. Eddy-hopping our way down the river, we scouted each rapid from our boats as the steep, ten-metre walls of the canyon offered no option of climbing up. The white water bubbled and laughed in some sections, and roared and howled in others. From a kayak, the power of white water is palpable, but also manageable with the right experience and know-how. Slowly making our way through the canyon downstream of the construction site, a chain of yellow, red, blue and green kayaks contrasted with the matt grey of the karst walls, and the sparkling blue and foaming white of the river. Butterflies and birds flickered overhead, trees and vines dripping off the steep walls, the electric green of foliage reflecting the fairy-tale blue of the water in the low-angle sunlight of the gorge. Gurgling streams trickled in, some spurting straight from the vertical stone walls like a tap, illustrating the mysterious and porous nature of limestone. As the incline mellowed out, we climbed out of kayaks and scrambled up the rounded, hip-like formations of limestone, sliding into massive bowls of rock that could hold five people, carved out by water moving stones in circular patterns for hundreds of years. Then we jumped into the deep pools to swim after our drifting boats. The water level was low, but not as low as it would be if this dam was built.

This is why we have come to the Valbona. To use striking kayaking footage from exploring unknown canyons and tributaries to communicate the sickening corruption-fuelled destruction of the last pristine ecosystems of Europe. And to give a voice to the locals fighting for these rivers. Direct actions like this one are BRD's speciality.

My introduction to activism started before I could walk or talk, attending protests from backpacks and strollers with my parents at home in Canada. My sisters and I attended actions against nuclear power, pollution and logging. In primary school, my mum pulled us from class to portage our canoe through the streets of downtown Toronto in protest of a mega highway through our favourite provincial park. But it wasn't until I was a teenager that I experienced the power, allure and thrill of white water, and at the same time, the fragility of wild rivers. After a month of canoeing the Rupert River in northern Ontario, I was tormented by the idea that the electricity I used to turn on lights at home was derived from the destruction of a river. As a university student I attended protests on Parliament Hill and participated in public meetings to keep a dam off the tributary of my home river. But after graduating university, my availability and motivation to speak out and act against injustice dwindled. I was passionate about rivers, but I didn't know how to transfer it into action, paralyzed by not knowing what to do, or how to start. I transitioned from a white-water canoe tripper to a freestyle kayaker, and became part of a party-hard, adrenaline-fuelled family of white-water worshippers – kayakers who revered rivers solely for their recreational value. Paddling was my top priority and signing an online petition became my pitiful attempt to protect the rivers I loved.

When I met the wild group of Slovenian kayakers, film-makers and photographers while working as the editor for a kayaking magazine, I jumped at the chance to get involved. Rok Rozman, the founder of BRD, a registered river conservation NGO in Slovenia, took the threat of over 3,000 dams planned for the rivers of his home personally, and combined white-water kayaking, science, film and direct action to protect the rivers of the Balkan Peninsula through protests, events and supporting locals fighting for their rivers. BRD's annual river conservation movement, Balkan Rivers Tour, blurs the line between paddling, protesting and storytelling by travelling to the Balkans to the community or area that needs the most support in defending local rivers. I became the communications manager of BRD and moved to Slovenia a year later. Over the past three years, our tight-knit group of kayakers turned river activists have spent hundreds of days in the Balkans, using our kayaks to raise awareness and using our cameras to tell the story of the locals' fight to protect the last wild rivers of Europe. Now, as part of a passionate tribe of kayakers who paddle with purpose, I can combine my profession as a freelance writer with my passion for nature conservation by working with BRD year-round, managing the NGO's communications and helping plan protests, events and actions.

———

As the sun crests the sharp limestone mountains, a warm glow forms, bringing out the details of the jagged teeth of the Albanian Alps. The soft light slides down the mountainside, illuminating a blanket of green formed by the forest of beech, pine and oak. In a cloud of dust, the clarity and peace of the moment is shattered. The waiting is over. The first construction trucks arrive, halting in front of us. We look to each other and link arms, creating a human chain that alternates between the kayakers' well-worn down jackets and pilled fleeces and the faux leather and thin windbreakers of the Valbona locals. No one says a word. The banner behind us speaks loud and clear: *Kur nuk ka shtet ka popull* (*When the state fails, the people enforce the law*). Earlier that month, the Albanian state court ruled that the construction of a hydro dam and the subsequent destruction of the river inside Valbona National Park is illegal. Yet the Albanian construction company continues to build, blasting stone and pouring concrete. So here we sit, physically blocking construction and sending our message: rivers are a common good, not a private commodity, and if the Albanian government will not enforce the law, this group of kayakers and locals will. Some of the workers wander around. Others pull out cell phones. We wait to see who will show up next.

Today, our kayaks don't see any white water. Stacked on the van, they are out of place against the backdrop of grey concrete and an almost dry riverbed. These boats represent our connection to rivers. With the ability to navigate technical and risky white water, I have explored the deep gorges and tight canyons of the Balkans that even locals, who have lived by the river for generations, have never experienced. This is a privilege and my motivation for standing up (or in this case, sitting down) for Balkan rivers, many of which still run unobstructed from snow line to seaside.

Kayaking, like all adventure sports, is a completely selfish endeavour. That is the main difference between sitting in the dust during a protest and sitting in a kayak in white water. But there are many similarities between organizing a protest and running a technical piece of white water. Both involve calculated risk and a high level of self-confidence. Especially here in the Balkans, where politics are laced with corruption and mafia. Kayaking and protesting involve significant planning – each protest performed must have a clear message, and each rapid navigated must have a clear line. We scout protest locations like we scout a rapid, with a plan A and B clearly delineated. Communication and trust are integral to both activities, so before each protest we gather as a group to go through actions and outcomes, ensuring everyone maintains a peaceful approach. And when things get crazy – in both kayaking and activism – it's key to keep your cool, right to the end.

For more than two hours we have been blocking the road and the sun is finally starting to warm us when two police cars arrive, followed shortly by a shiny SUV carrying two men in button-up shirts and expensive watches. Even without the whispered translation from my Albanian comrades, I follow the tone and theme of the interaction: the businessmen are angry and want the police to remove us physically. They are furious that a bunch of kayakers sitting in the dirt are stronger than their trucks. The businessmen shout, point and threaten us in English and Albanian. Only one of us stands, an Aussie kayaker who calmly displays the court order stating the construction is illegal.

The veins in the businessman's neck bulge as he yells, "Five minutes! You have five minutes to move before you go to jail!" He swivels and points directly at a woman in a yellow sundress with wild, auburn hair. "Starting with you!"

Her response is unusually bold for a Valbona Valley resident. She snorts, snickers and smiles. Catherine Bohne is a foreigner-local hybrid. After visiting the Valbona 13 years ago, she sold her small Manhattan bookshop and moved to Albania permanently. She married a local, and together they started a small resort and campsite along the river. When dynamite and diggers started construction of the hydropower dam without local consultation, Catherine mobilized the community and registered an NGO to fight for the rights of the river and the locals. She laughs now because her American citizenship grants her a kind of immunity. After over two years of fighting in courtrooms and on the computer, she turns to us and says, "A few days in jail would be like a holiday for me."

Catherine is seen as the brave leader of this movement, but she isn't the only woman fighting for rivers in the Balkans. In a region of the world known for male dominance and masculine attitudes, I've noticed that people fighting for rivers are predominately female. In almost every side valley or village that the BRD visits, it's women who are the driving force of river conservation, challenging corruption and standing up for Mother Earth. Much like the minority ladies in white-water kayaking, women here are used to playing in a man's world. We use our minds over muscles, and use empathy and emotion to conquer fear. Staring up at the businessmen shouting threats at us, I imagine what the inside of an Albanian jail cell looks like. But then I think of the brave women of the Balkans who I have met through river conservation. Women like environmental lawyer Alexandra Bujaroska, who wears red high heels in the courtrooms of North Macedonia, where she defends the wild rivers of her country. Or Slovenia's Neza Posnjak, an endless source of information on legislation and the policy of freshwater conservation in Slovenia. Nataša Crnković puts her life at risk by speaking up in the media and organizing street protests in defence of rivers in Bosnia and Herzegovina. And the committed and courageous ladies of the Kruščica River, who formed a 400-day bridge blockade preventing construction workers from continuing construction on a hydropower plant that would divert their drinking water into pipes.

The ladies boldly fighting for the rivers of the Balkans defy cultural norms. Locals are often shocked to see a female white-water kayaking the rivers here, but floating down a rapid in a kayak is a frivolous activity and unfair comparison to what these women are doing. They are much tougher than I am. Tough here means surviving trauma and loss during times of war. It means growing, gathering and providing food for your family. It means standing up for your rivers when physical abuse and jail time are a reality. It means staring greed, bulldozers and politicians in the eye.

———

Catherine remains on the ground, arms linked with a kayaker on one side and a local on the other. Despite the threats and demands of the businessmen, the police officers take no action, confirming that our law enforcement action is working. Word of the blockade spreads to the nearby town of Bajram Curri and a TV crew arrives. The presence of mainstream media diffuses the tension and the protest loses its edge slightly. But it also elevates our blockade from a risk to a success. I watch the TV host interviewing a village elder, his white, bell-shaped moustache dancing while he speaks in the slow clucks and "shhs" of Albania's beautiful language. Eventually, Catherine stands, brushes dust from her bare, goosebump-covered legs and addresses the TV cameras, confidently answering in fluent Albanian. She ends the interview in tears after describing what the Valbona means to her. Courage and emotion go hand in hand when fighting for the wild rivers of the Balkans.

The construction trucks have long since driven away and the businessmen disappeared the moment the TV cameras arrived. The police remain, but the stand-off is over. We won this battle. The war, however, will continue in the courtrooms and offices across Albania. The 8 p.m. news will tell today's story. And in magazines, online publications and through social media outlets we will tell the story of the Valbona, and other rivers threatened by unnecessary hydro dams. We will continue to remind people that being out in the environment doesn't make you an environmentalist; that if you ski, climb, paddle or play in the wilderness, you have a duty to take action to protect it. Again and again we will pose the question: to whom do our natural resources and wild places belong? Corporations, governments and multinational institutions? Or all of us? BRD will continue to challenge paddlers and people to think for themselves. A forest, mountain or river shouldn't be regarded in terms of human values and experiences. It should be valued as its own entity.

Energized, inspired, relieved... and quite stiff, we leave our sentry, visions of a warm fire and cosy sleeping bags tempting us back to our campsite upstream. We know our impact today is minimal, and that this is just one day in a long battle to save this river. But the hours spent as a part of this chain of defiance, the relationships formed with locals, the energy of disobedience and the pleasure of watching locals in front of TV cameras have fuelled our collective desire to continue helping to defend rivers.

Through the paddling and protesting actions of BRD I have discovered a paddle can be a powerful tool. By pairing a paddle with a pen, or a camera and a kayak, we have found a way to do our part to fight for the last free-flowing rivers of Europe and to contribute to global river conservation. And along the way, we are enjoying wild white water in some of the most remote and beautiful rivers of the world – from Bulgaria to Bosnia, Croatia to Montenegro, Slovenia to Serbia. With today as proof, Balkan River Defence demonstrates that creativity, resistance and community can stop the destruction of wilderness so that some of the world's rivers will continue to flow wild and free from the mountains to the sea.

Sonam, a Tibetan nomad on the Chang Tang Plateau

THE LAST OF
THE NOMADS
CAT VINTON

Cat Vinton is an award-winning adventure and ethnographic photographer with a curiosity for the people who roam the furthest corners of the earth.

She lives with nomadic families, documenting their extraordinary resilience and self-sufficiency in their relentlessly challenged existence. This intimacy has allowed her to capture the human spirit, survival stories and the fragile connection between people and land. Since 2007, Cat has completed five solo expeditions to the nomadic Sámi, Mongolian, Dolpo, Moken and Tibetan people.

She also documents expeditions, artists' work and a myriad of projects across the globe. Cat joined Aliénor le Gouvello on her epic adventure crossing Australia along the Great Dividing Range with three wild horses, and in 2019 Cat embarked on a five-month journey into China's remotest mountains, exploring the diverse ethnic minorities. A book Cat worked on with the children of a remote island in the Mergui Archipelago is now sold to people exploring the region, with all proceeds going directly to the village. She has been published in *National Geographic* online, *The Guardian*, *Sidetracked Magazine*, *Survival International* and *Oceanographic Magazine* (among others); her images have been published in a number of books.

Find out more about Cat at:
W: www.maptia.com/catvinton
& www.catvphotography.co.uk
& www.illuminate.org.uk
I: @catvinton

Adventure is a path. Real adventure – self-determined, self-motivated, often risky – forces you to have first-hand encounters with the world. The world the way it is, not the way you imagine it. Your body will collide with the earth and you will bear witness. In this way you will be compelled to grapple with the limitless kindness and bottomless cruelty of humankind – and perhaps realize that you yourself are capable of both. This will change you. Nothing will ever again be black-and-white.

The Ghost Road by Mark Jenkins

I smiled at Tashi on the first day. She beamed back, shy and beautiful. The second day we drank Tibetan tea and she showed me precious turquoise and rare red coral, which she sells on her tiny street stall. On the third day (it must have been somewhere below minus ten) she asked if I'd like to go to her home (in the Tibetan refugee camp) to warm by the fire and eat with her and her husband. This is where it began.

I had arrived in Leh as the season had come to a close. The cold had set in and snow had already fallen. The small town had ground to the slow pace of winter. Mountain-framed – at an altitude of over 3,500 metres – *stupas* and whitewashed houses make up the old town, full of life and smiles.

Tashi had some broken English, picked up on the street from selling her Tibetan jewellery. Showing her images from my research of where I wanted to go, the faces and way of life I was hoping to find, we start to hatch a plan. A friendship is happening fast – we are the same age – we'd already smiled and hugged and felt a connected spirit. I've persuaded her to close her small stall, and to accompany me into the coming winter months high on the Chang Tang plateau, in search of the last Tibetan nomads. Returning to her roots.

We rattle over the rugged peaks of this stunning, wild, remote landscape of the high Himalaya – in a truck open to the biting wind. Crammed full of Tibetan faces of all ages, covered in layers of skins and colour, I found myself in the middle of these curious, shy, beautiful people. Dressed in a Tibetan wool *chuba* (a Tibetan coat), my right arm free (worn as they do), my dark hair, tanned cheeks and grin just about merge me into the mass of people and get me through the military checks and free onto the Chang Tang plateau – on the Indian side of the border.

Finally, after a few long days crossing this frozen land, we reach a small Tibetan camp of yak-haired tents wedged in between jagged peaks. One side India, the other side Tibet (the Tibetan Autonomous Region, as the Chinese call it). It's already dusk and the temperature has plummeted. A distant relative of Tashi's (a widowed man) invites us into his small tent. We huddle round his warm stove with bleating baby goats, share tea and exchange childlike excitement at this unexpected encounter. Tashi and he hardly pause for breath as they talk into the late hours. I drift off into a sound sleep.

That first morning, out early, I met Sonam, collecting water at the frozen river. We had witnessed the first rays of sun rip through the rugged mountainscape. The years on her face seem more than her actual twelve. Her eyes sparkled, wide and inquisitive. She seemed compelled to watch my every move across her frozen landscape. Every glimpse of each other – our smile connected. We seemed to lock in to a mutual fascination.

It was bitterly cold. The mountains already seized by winter. From December until spring, an intense and extreme cold paralyzes the region, isolating the people here from the rest of the country.

Sonam sees me really cold and beckons me to her home – a black yak-haired tent on the edge of the camp, somehow nestled into sheer rock. This becomes home for my winter stay on the Chang Tang plateau with Tashi, Sonam's father Gaysto, mother Yangyen and their family.

Completely immersed in their daily life, eating everything they do, and sleeping side by side, under layers of skins. Moving at their pace, I shadow their days, witnessing the hardship of survival in this high-altitude existence that shapes those who call it home.

Life's rhythm here is in tune with the needs of their livestock. Their herd of sheep, goats and yak are their lifeline – their welfare is paramount, and crucial to nomadic survival. Sonam leads their sheep and goats across the silent white mountains in search of grazing land. Out from dawn to dusk every day, singing to her four-legged friends, seemingly content, alone all day in the wilds of the winter elements. Her cheeks cracked and scorched red, smeared with yak butter in an attempt to protect them from the bitter wind.

The yak is imperative to existence and survival, providing food, milk and butter – doubling as sunscreen. Skins softened and stitched into incredible *chubas* and warm winter boots. The yak hair is hand-spun, making wool, and takes about a year to weave into a tent – the nomads' home. Chunks of bone become adornments for the women's hair, and are played with as a game by the young children. Even the tail is used as a brush to sweep their home floor. The yaks transport the nomads' life belongings as they migrate in search of new pastures, with the shift of seasons, across this wild land.

No trees mark this high Himalayan scene – yet fire is essential to survive the forty-below temperatures that frequent these months of winter. Yangyen carves out patterns with the yak dung in the fresh snow every morning at first light. Once dried, this becomes the fuel for the stove – winter's lifeline, which she tends day and night. This is all knowledge that's taken thousands of years to evolve and pass down through generations. Their ancestors are the spirits of these mountains, the sky and the rivers.

I came to intimately know their long days, navigating each of their roles in this unforgiving terrain, each imperative to survival. Fighting the bitter cold – my fingers and toes already damaged from months in frozen lands before now. Life is not easy here, living on the edge of existence.

This is not their homeland. These nomads are refugees in the Indian Himalaya. They come from the other side of the peaks – the Tibetan side. Sixty years ago, under the cover of winter darkness, Sonam's father Gaysto, then a boy of seven, walked for weeks to flee the Chinese invasion. Both his and Yangyen's family had made this perilous journey after their spiritual leader, His Holiness the Dalai Lama, had been forced to flee his homeland.

Every step of the experience is marked in his memory. He recounts in a soft voice, with glazed eyes. His ultimate wish had been to return to his sacred Tibetan homeland, his landscape of lost dreams. (Sadly, he never made it. But I hope now his spirit has returned.)

It's incredible to share life alongside these people – who know how to navigate the mountains, who know how to survive in their remote peaks. Who for generations have forged a way of life in rhythm with the seasons, who have a profound respect and intimate connection with this harsh, wild landscape and with the animals and plants of the natural world.

———

Across the globe, lost land, stolen by imposed borders, has forced apart those who've called it home and who've nurtured it for thousands of years. Aggressive governments are shaping the future of these wild lands, causing environmental ruin.

Climate change is playing its part too in the upheaval of human and planetary existence. Weather patterns have become unpredictable and fierce. It's those who have made the least impact on the climate who are suffering the most.

Spending time with indigenous people has taught me that wealth and success are not measured in belongings and status, but in the strength of our human spirit.

For the last few years I've not called one place home. Instead I've roamed, weaving my life and work, more in tune with a wilder spirit and those who still live connected to nature. This freedom keeps me healthy and strong. I am happiest being outside and on the move.

From the High Himalaya to the Arctic Circle, the Gobi Desert to the Andaman Sea, I have followed a passion, documenting the last of the nomadic people who still roam free, immersed in the natural world.

Across these diverse landscapes and cultures, I have witnessed many common strands in the nomadic existence – spiritual and physical; in survival and resilience.

―――――

Roaming wild across the great Central Asian plains and mountain ranges of Mongolia, escorting hundreds of wild horses, sheep, goats and camels to their autumn pastures, these residents of the vast open steppe of an ancient land are the nomads of the south Gobi Desert.

It took me three days to persuade them. I wanted to feel the energy and spirit, the power of thundering hooves, of wild horses charging free across the land. I lay in the dirt, on my front, a horseman straddling my body while two others charged their herd toward me in a whirlwind of dust and deafening power. They had, as I had confidently (uncertainly) predicted, been scared of what lay in their path, and as they got close, they split and thundered past me on both sides. My camera jammed with the dust, but not before I'd captured it.

"A man without a horse is like a bird without wings" – Mongolian proverb.

―――――

Nomadic people have the lightest touch on the earth – they move, which allows the land and seas to recover. They leave no trace and they survive on only what they need, without greed.

The mountains and the oceans are where my heart beats loudest.

Every other breath we take depends on the ocean; the tides have shaped our continents, given character to our coastlines, and over time have isolated islands from the land.

The islands of the Mergui Archipelago and the crystal waters that shape them are special. These 800 islands in the Andaman Sea are home to a nomadic sea culture, its people roaming these waters for centuries, weaving across the Thai–Burmese border that lies invisible in the sea. The tidal rhythm here moves in aquamarine, cyan and turquoise – across white sand beaches that reach the edge of the rainforest.

Nestled in a tight row, we all stir as the first light reflects off the calm water, dancing on the roof of the *kabang* (a traditional wooden Moken boat), as the gentle low voices of Tat and Sabai drift into focus. This is how the days began, living with the nomadic Moken.

It had taken me over a month to find them. The flotillas of *kabang* were already long gone. But Tat and Sabai had managed to cling on to their nomadic existence, on one of the last *kabang* still at sea. The Moken are said to have migrated from southern China, over 4,000 years ago, making a life at sea. The *kabang* is at the heart of their culture – symbolizing freedom – and had formed the currency of Moken society.

The rains had passed and the dry season returned, rendering freedom back to Tat and Sabai on their *kabang*. I was witnessing some of the last years of the nomadic Moken way of life.

Sabai is incredibly beautiful. Her slight frame hides her strength. She stands proud, with the warmest smile. Her energy is slightly childlike, even mischievous – our locked smiles acknowledge our similar spirit, a connection without need of a common language.

Sabai was born on a *kabang* – it's the only life she knows; a life shaped by the tides, the seasons, the myths and the spirits. Roaming these seas, rotating their hunting ground, navigating the waters and the hundreds of islands that make up "home". Home to the world's last sea nomads – these softly-treading hunter-gatherers have lived this way for generations.

The days had rhythm but not routine. We didn't eat three times a day but instead when we had a fresh catch. Daylight was the only mark of time. They don't count their years. They have no notion or measure of time.

The Moken – meaning "people immersed in water" – learn to swim before they walk. Their spirit resonates with the turtle, who they believe are their spiritual "sisters" – as the myths and legends go – needing both the sea and land to survive. The Moken people can hold their breath longer, can see further and have vision that's sharper underwater than almost any other people on earth.

Sabai had intuitively understood my curiosity of their life at the water's edge, and was sharing with me the ways of the Moken. In awe, I began to intimately know how they live in rhythm with this pristine seascape. Sabai was the gatherer: she'd chase crabs in the rocks at low tide, coax the lobsters from tiny holes on the seabed with a small bait fish hanging from bamboo-made string dangling in arm's-length water. She'd move the water in a way the sea urchin's spikes would mimic. As the spikes lay flattened, she'd prise them from the water. Using her fingers, she'd eat this delicacy raw and in the moment. I watched her skilfully catch eels in the warm shallow waters and fill her handwoven rattan basket with huge clams, mussels and other delicacies I'd not seen before. At the fringes of the rainforest she'd dig holes a metre deep, searching for wild yams. Back on the white sand beach, she'd burn huge chunks of wood, in already-high humid temperatures, seemingly unfazed by the heat. Once fully in flames, she'd bury the burning wood deep in the sand – she was making charcoal for her small stove on the *kabang*, where she'd cook all this fresh catch from the sea and its shores. This intimate knowledge of a nomadic way of life – in the last years.

So many of my days were spent watching Tat dropping through the clear blue of the Andaman Sea, on a single breath, hunting fish, leaping with force from the *kabang* with his harpoon and pinpoint accuracy.

Or from the shallow waters, barely rippling the surface, he'd send his spear into a shoal of fish or an unsuspecting eagle ray. The ocean is their home, and they are as much a part of its rhythm as the fish they've always hunted.

Three of Tat and Sabai's boys lived this free life at sea on the *kabang* (only four of their eleven children had survived). Tat taught them how to hunt fish, how to freedive with a spear and a harpoon, how to gut and prepare the fish and how to sail the *kabang*. They'd learn from Tat's drafted illustrations in the sand, immersed and involved from their earliest days. Today the boys help make strips of bamboo into rope (kway), stitching pandanus leaves to craft a new roof for the *kabang*. These are the last Moken children to live this life at sea.

They were always on the move. Days came in and out of the water and the land. They understood the unpredictability of the sea, and their delicate place within it. But life had changed for Tat and Sabai. It was harder to find food – they'd become the very last family to live this nomadic existence, and they'd become lonely.

A Moken myth warns of "laboon" – the seventh wave. Elders have carried this mythical tale through the generations, warning that when it comes they should head to the mountains or deep water. This led them to survive the devastating tsunami of 2004, despite them lying directly in its path. Only a few Moken elders are left to pass on traditional knowledge, and the myths and legends of their spiritual world, carried on the wind in whispered voices of times long gone.

I returned a few years later to find my Moken family when I heard Sabai had lost her sight, and that their nomadic life had become too difficult alone, forcing them to land. I will never forget the image of Tat, that day, as he walked toward me, with silent tears, empty eyes and a lost spirit, his hands crossed in front of his chest indicating his vanished freedom – his life changed forever. I left with the heaviest heart – seeing them fragile, lost and disconnected from the only life they knew.

My images of their nomadic days had become overnight an important visual legacy of a way of life, not only for the future generations, who may never experience this existence, but also as a memory of those nomadic days for Tat and Sabai and their boys – being free.

Again I returned to the Andaman Sea. They were stronger – part of their spirit had returned. They've found a place in their now-settled existence. Sabai sings again and Tat has found his way back out to sea, to hunt fish with his harpoon. The boys (now teenagers) are forging their own path, moving away from Tat's traditional way of life. But they have the knowledge of the old ways, everything they've learned and experienced from Tat and Sabai, the *kabang* and the spirit of the sea – it's in their blood. Teenagers can be difficult, lost between childhood and adulthood, working out who they are, growing and searching, but these young people have a confidence and calm, a strong understanding of their place and of who they are.

The Moken spirit is very much alive.

———

I have learned so much about the importance and the purpose of life – a moral and ethical code – from the nomadic people of the world's remote corners. About survival and the fragile connection between people and nature. Their lives a tale of strength, resilience, dedication, belief, resistance and evolution.

Photography is my part in the storytelling of life – with the hope of encouraging people to reconnect to the land and community, and to be a part of protecting our natural world and all the ways of life that coexist.

I have learned to trust my intuition. It has been my guide. Passion and curiosity have ruled my heart, with empathy at my core.

Being immersed in life – alongside people whose narrative is still written by nature, rooted in ancestral knowledge – is my inspiration.

Our choices define us and our place in the world. Being in the elements is where I find my energy and my balance, giving me a sense of purpose.

The kindness, generosity and openness of the people I've been lucky enough to meet, become friends with, learn from and live alongside – are etched in my heart.

Thank you to all those people who have "let me in" to their lives and shared with me who they are – an incredible honour. You are treasured.

SOAKING UP THE LANDSCAPE

EMILY CHAPPELL

Emily Chappell is an author, adventurer and advocate from Mid Wales, whose bicycle journeys have taken her across several continents. She has written two books: *What Goes Around* documents her years as a London cycle courier, and *Where There's A Will* follows her into the world of ultra-distance bicycle racing.

I was nervous about riding with Isla, but relieved when she volunteered to take charge of route planning, and also amused when she issued a disclaimer a few days before we set off.

"This type of 'cycling' may involve:

- A lot of walking
- Wet feet
- Tracks on the map that don't actually exist on the ground
- River crossings"

The plan was to meet at my place in Mid Wales and ride to the coast, 30 miles away, where we'd spend the night and then ride back the following day. After the tussocky exertions of the Bear Bones 200 the previous weekend – where I'd covered 124 miles in 19 hard-won hours, through the worst of Mid Wales' mud, peat and slurry – this looked like it would be the *right* sort of weekend ride, with cafe stops, reasonable mileage, and possibly even fish and chips at the end. Despite her disclaimer, Isla assured me that we'd "go slow" and "soak up the landscape", lulling me into what turned out to be an entirely false sense of security.

We set off into gentle rain, optimistically reminding each other that the forecast had been "patchy" and hoping that we might be lucky enough to ride into the right patches.

Less than 3 miles in, things started to get interesting. Isla led me off the usual well-trodden route into my local town, along a forestry track and out across a muddy field. A rainbow appeared. And I got my first puncture.

Tempting though it was to walk the few hundred yards into town and fix it over a coffee, we agreed that we hadn't quite covered enough distance yet, so I hastily replaced the tube, realizing in the process that I'd left my second spare on the kitchen table and so had only one.

Ten minutes later we turned on to another muddy bridleway, smelled the tell-tale scent of freshly cut hawthorn and a moment later heard a malevolent hiss from my back tyre. But the sun was now edging its way through the clouds and our spirits were high, so we laughed as I flipped the bike, and Isla offered to patch my spare tube while I wiped my muddy hands on my shorts and set about replacing the holey one.

We left the floodplain and found ourselves ascending an ancient drovers' road, sunk deep into the landscape between two hedgerows, with autumnal trees clasping hands above us, so that we climbed into a tunnel of gold and amber, shafts of sunshine dappling us as our feet and tyres squelched through the mud.

Another puncture. This time it was Isla's, which made me feel slightly better. We stopped under a shower of hawthorn berries to fix it and found ourselves still smiling, as the red fruit glowed above us in the sun, and we looked back down the hill on a view of my town I'd never seen before. So far, we had averaged one puncture every 2 miles, but we weren't in any hurry, after all, and we had the whole day to get ourselves to Borth, which really wasn't all that far away.

I had, of course, reckoned without Isla's route planning, which largely eschewed tarmac, and sent us straight over the hills, on winding forestry roads and vertiginous singletrack, frequently obliging us to get off and push or carry our bikes through knee-deep peat bog.

"So this was what she meant by 'soaking up the landscape'," I thought to myself, as cold brown water seeped into my shoes and I spied a river up ahead, with large stone piles separated by 5 metres of empty air, whatever bridged them existing only in memory or ambition.

Our river-crossing tactics differed. Isla triumphantly produced a pair of Crocs from her pannier, whereas I just stripped off overshoes, shoes and socks, and went in barefoot, holding my breath as I slid and stumbled across the stony riverbed. The water was cold enough to sting, but once I'd fumbled my damp socks and muddy shoes back on, I found that my feet were glowing and tingling deliciously. Perhaps river crossings weren't so bad.

We emerged into civilization briefly at lunchtime and spent an hour or so being regarded with curiosity and disgust by the other patrons of the Hafod Hotel at Devil's Bridge, most of whom seemed to be out for a sedate Saturday drive and hadn't an ounce of mud on them. We patched our muddy tubes at the table, wolfed down our chips and paninis, insisted they refill our teapots and then were on our way, speeding down through still-green woods into a steep-sided valley, where a narrow-gauge railway overlooked a broad, brown river.

We squinted through the reflection of the sky on the water, trying to ascertain the size of the rocks beneath and whether we might reasonably expect to ride through, then inevitably erred on the side of caution, and once again sat down to take off our shoes and socks. A stony track crept up the other side of the valley, through yellowing trees shaggy with moss, then reached a small white cottage and abruptly turned into a footpath, slicing up through ancient woodlands. At one point it bisected another old drovers' road, set deep into the hillside, lined with trees that perhaps were once hedges, and recalled long-ago journeys made by people no one now remembers, for purposes at which we could only guess.

Centuries ago, I realized, this road wouldn't have been seen as the back route or footpath (or overgrown gully) it is today – it would have been a highway as much as any other, and those who trudged along it would have had none of the sense we had, of the way being slow and stumbling, since this was the only way they had of moving. Although both Isla and I unquestionably prefer cycling (and even pushing, as we were now) to driving or sitting on a train, we had still undertaken this journey on the understanding that it would be slow and occasionally frustrating. "If we manage five miles an hour, we'll be doing well," she'd warned me at the start, and we couldn't help but compare it, even subconsciously, even unfavourably, to the smoothness and effortlessness of travelling along a tarmacked road or of gazing through a train window as busy rails chattered beneath us.

A couple of hundred years ago, human beings had no concept of that type of movement – or even of the freedom and exhilaration of a bicycle. They would have trudged patiently up the hillsides through muddy leaves churned up by the feet of their livestock, hauling their loads over rocks and intervening roots, covering just a few miles every day. The paved road we'd briefly followed into Devil's Bridge would have been as alien to them as the surface of Mars.

A little further on, I glanced down the hillside and happened to see the roof of a very old car, half-buried in the undergrowth, broken and crumpled, with weeds growing out of its windows. Someone must have pushed it off the top of the hill, many years previously, either as the culmination of a drunken joyride or just as a way of disposing of unwanted property. I imagined the great disturbance it must have made as it ripped its way down the hillside, finally coming to rest against a few straining tree trunks, and realized that this was not only a place that pre-dated the motor vehicle – it was also a place that would continue to exist and slowly evolve long after all cars are consigned to the scrapheap, and the way we move through the landscape has changed once again.

A couple of hours later, after following the fire roads through the Nant yr Arian trail centre and skirting a lake, we found ourselves thundering along another stony track, glancing repeatedly over to our right where an enormous fold of rock thrust up out of the valley, signalling the beginning of Snowdonia and speaking of a violent landscape that predated even our ancient drovers' roads. We raced our bikes headlong toward the sea, the sinking sun and the hot dinner that surely awaited us, exuberant that our end was in sight, yet also anxious to rest and recover, knowing that the following day would be even slower, damper and tougher.

"I think at this point we're about as far as you can get from a road, almost anywhere in the British Isles," Isla announced a day later.

I felt my now customary mixture of fear and excitement. We were pushing (and occasionally carrying) our bikes along a wide valley, carpeted with golden grass whose pale-green roots were occasionally exposed by the rustling wind, and which fell away at the summits of the nearby peaks, revealing craggy grey rocks. On Isla's map, a bridleway was marked with a bold green line, but here on the ground there was nothing at all – nothing but acres of unrideable tussocks, here and there interspersed with rusty looking peat bogs into which we'd sink up to our knees. We had long ago given up trying to keep our shoes dry.

The weather had finally taken a turn for the worse and a thick grey cloud was rolling along the valley behind us, occasionally flinging us a scattering of raindrops as a warning of what was to come. Isla's legs were tired. My hands were sore. Both of us were keeping our hunger at bay with handfuls of sweets, knowing that our calorie deficit was growing by the minute. Our shorts were caked in mud, our socks were squelching and our noses were running uncontrollably. And we still hadn't stopped smiling.

Every now and then the line on Isla's Garmin would lead us on to a sheep track, and for a minute or so we'd get back on our bikes and whoop as we pedalled along the rim of the valley, momentarily confident that we now had a path, and surely that would lead to a track, which would lead to a road, which would, eventually, lead to civilization, people, houses, warm beds, and the moment when we could look back on all of this and laugh. But then the track would disappear, the sheep having evidently decided that it wasn't worthwhile breaking their way through all of those tussocks after all, and we'd heave the bikes back on to our shoulders and laugh anyway.

Far, far away, at the end of the valley, we could see a stone building – unquestionably abandoned, but nonetheless encouraging, because it suggested that humans had been here, had considered the place accessible enough to live and work in, and had managed to haul in several tonnes of stone, meaning there had to be some sort of track. But at our slow, arrhythmic pace, the tiny edifice kept its distance, and it was over an hour before we eventually climbed a fence, crossed one more river and laboured our way up the final slope to a flat, grassy ledge. It had looked from a distance like it might be a track, but it turned out to be an ancient drystone wall now overgrown with grass and moss, buried in the landscape like the old car we'd seen the previous afternoon.

We stumbled along the wall for a few more minutes, slowly climbing up the side of the valley as the sky darkened and the rain began to fall in earnest. Finally, the track we'd feared we might never find lay ahead of us, and we got back on our bikes and accelerated toward civilization, my log-burner and Isla's train home, our fingers twitching and cramping on our brake levers, our socks squelching inside our sodden shoes as we pedalled – and both of us still smiling.

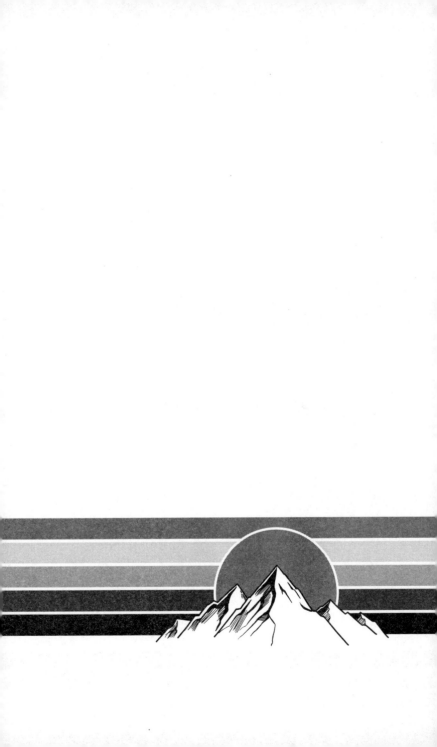

CLIMB EVERY MOUNTAIN

EMMA SVENSSON

Emma Svensson is a freelance fashion photographer who abandoned her life in Stockholm to live in her van and climb mountains. She started doing photography, shooting rockstars, at a young age, and started an agency for concert photography photos at the age of 19. She has been an important voice for equality in the photography world in Sweden all her life. She runs her own production company, coaches and teaches photography in her own master-classes, and tries to use her platforms to help and inspire others to live their dreams. She started climbing mountains just three years ago and now it has taken over her life. She is looking forward to future expeditions and projects – her goal is to inspire others to realize that you don't have to be a professional athlete to do these things.

Find out more about Emma at:
I: @emmasvenssonphoto
F: Photographer Emma Svensson

I was on a plane to New Zealand to do a photography tour and somewhere between Bangkok and Sydney I decided to watch a movie. I flicked through the selection and decided on *Everest*, a true story about Rob Hall and Scott Fischer's expedition to the highest mountain in the world in 1996 where things didn't end too well. In fact, most people died, including the legendary guides. So, when I thought "I have to start climbing mountains" after seeing this movie, it's not the reaction most people have. But for me it was a life-changing experience. Like, overwhelming. Love at first sight. Bigger than anything else. I had only felt like this once before in my life and that was when I photographed my first concert at age 19. That made me become a photographer. And now, here I was on a plane with my heart beating so hard and hands shaking because I knew: I had to climb Everest (8,848 metres).

Growing up in the forest in Sweden, I didn't really have access to mountains. In fact, I had only climbed one mountain a few years before – Galdhøpiggen (2,469 metres), the highest mountain in Norway. I was a real couch potato back then and it was the hardest thing I had ever done. When I got to the top, totally exhausted, I couldn't even enjoy the amazing view. I was finished. Going down was so painful on my knees. My legs stopped working. I sat on a rock for 45 minutes crying because I didn't know how to get down. I had to pretend

I was being chased by wolves to get some adrenalin to be able to keep going. And when that finished it was almost dark and my friend basically had to carry me down. We lost the trail, ended up in some bushes and I gave up on ever coming back down alive. When we finally got down 12 hours after we started, I promised myself I would never, ever climb a mountain again.

And here I was: 34 years old, just about to get married, totally out of shape, with no experience and all I wanted was to climb mountains because I watched a movie about it. When I told my fiancé about my dreams he thought it was a really bad idea and that someone like me couldn't do something like that.

I forgot about the mountains and got married instead. It was an amazing wedding. Three days in an old train station building in the Swedish countryside. Over 200 guests. Everyone was there. It was the best party of my life. I was, after all, marrying a DJ. We had been together for five years and during these years I had also been a bonus mom to his kid. We lived a typical city life in Stockholm. I worked as a fashion photographer and was running my own production company in Sweden with 12 employees. My life was a mix between hard work, family life and fashion events.

I also arranged photography tours all over the world and a few weeks after our wedding I was away on one of those in the US. At the end of the trip something started to feel weird. I couldn't tell what it was, but as soon as I came back home I was met at the door with the words "we need to talk". And you know that is never good. My legs were shaking. I felt nauseous. Frozen on the inside. I could not breathe. We sat down on our sofa and he told me he no longer wanted to be with me. My biggest nightmare became true. The worst thing that could ever happen to me happened. The man I had just married had dumped me six weeks after our wedding.

I was totally destroyed. Heartbroken. Sad. I didn't know how to be alive. I didn't eat. I didn't sleep. But somewhere in all of this I decided not to become an angry and bitter person. I wanted to see this as an opportunity to do everything I had always wanted to do. To follow my dreams. I started thinking about the mountains again and booked myself a spot on an expedition to climb the highest mountain in the US outside Alaska – Mount Whitney (4,421 metres) in California – via a mountaineers' route a few months later. It was an amazing experience. I really enjoyed it and a few months after that I climbed Mount Toubkal (4,167 metres), the highest mountain in Morocco.

But it was not until the following summer that everything went crazy. I climbed Mount Elbrus (5,642 metres) in Russia, the highest mountain in Europe, and stood on the summit on 1 August 2017. It was a hard climb from the north side. I was totally exhausted going down. At one point I laid down on the glacier and said: "I can't take one more step." My guide, a super-cool Russian girl named Xenia, told me to get up and go back down to high camp. Somehow, I managed to stumble down to the barrack and crash into my bed. I woke up a few hours later, glad to still be alive.

When I got back home a few days later I was restless. I needed a new goal. A new project. I had climbed the highest mountain in Europe. What if I was going to climb the highest mountain in every country in Europe? Could a regular girl like me even do something like that? Which mountains are even the highest ones? How difficult are they? I did 2 hours of research on Google and then I decided to go for it! Just like that. Spontaneous and crazy, maybe, and with very bad timing. It was the end of the climbing season. I had no money saved for something like this and no time either. My schedule was packed with photoshoots in the upcoming weeks.

But I just had to do this.

And, to make it even harder for myself, I decided to put a time limit on it and do it in less than one year. I found out months later there was a world record for doing this and that was two and a half years.

I made a list of all the mountains I was going to climb. I counted 49. I used the same list as the others who had taken this on before. The guy with the world record only climbed 43 mountains. I made a careful plan of what mountain to climb on what day. I was going to rent a car and drive around Europe before winter to tick off as many as possible from my list. I was eager to start, but had to wait a few weeks before I could go on my mountain tour. There was just one thing I had to do first...

I had to go climb Mont Blanc (4,810 metres). Because as a regular girl with very limited climbing experience, I knew no one would take me seriously if I told them about my project. They would think I was crazy – and I probably was. I needed it to be a little bit more legit. And I needed to test myself, too, to see if I would have a chance to pull this off. So, I booked a guide – 63-year-old Sandy Allan from Scotland – and met up with him in Chamonix for my climb.

"Are you fit?" he asked me.

"Not sure," I said. It was the truth. I wasn't really fit enough for this challenge. But it never bothered me. I was thinking that I would become fit while doing it.

Someone said climbing a mountain is 40 per cent physical, 40 per cent mental and 20 per cent circumstances. I believe that is pretty accurate.

The last stretch to the summit of Mont Blanc was very, very hard. But I did it! We were very lucky with the weather and by sunrise we were standing on the top of the highest mountain in western Europe. I could not have been more happy. Even if it was a struggle, it was proof that maybe I had a chance of doing this.

A few weeks later I rented a car in Milan and drove to Liechtenstein to climb Grauspitz (2,599 metres). My plan was to climb as many of the mountains around the Alps as possible before bad weather and winter arrived. It was already mid-September and looking up at the mountain massif I did not even know which peak to climb. This was my first climb without a guide. I had to google it on the way up. Not the peak with the iron cross. Not the peak with the white cross either. The one between. But how the hell do you get there? Grauspitz was almost never climbed so there was no trail to the top. Fresh snow had made it more difficult, according to the old man running the Älplibahn lift, who thought it was a bad idea for me to go there. "Try another peak instead, something easier." But for me there was only one peak I wanted to climb now and looking up at it I had no idea how to get there, but I knew I had to try.

The higher I got, the worse the rock got. Rotten. Falling apart under my feet. Slippery. Wet. Snow and ice. It was the scariest ever. You don't want to fall here. I was all alone on the mountain. Two days before two guys had climbed it, the old man told me. When I got to the foot of the mountain, I saw their tracks in the snow. It gave me courage to continue. It was steep, but the fresh snow made it possible without too much trouble. From my research I knew there was a false summit and that the real summit was a little bit tricky. It demanded a down climb and an exposed traverse. Not long, but long enough to scare off the two men from two days before. Their tracks ended at the false summit. I knew I had to continue. I walked very carefully. One step at the time. Trying to be as safe as possible. On both sides it dropped a few hundred metres. If you lost your balance here, it would mean death. I thought about my mum. She would not approve of this. But I got to the top unscathed.

A quick summit selfie later and I was on my way back down.

Next on my list was the highest mountain in Germany, Zugspitze (2,962 metres), but as soon as I got there with my Italian rental car a big snowstorm totally destroyed my amazing schedule. It would not be possible to climb anything in the Alps for the rest of the year.

I had to improvise and make a new plan. I drove to Monaco and climbed some stairs (161 metres) to the highest point in the city state. To Spain (Mulhacén, 3,479 metres) and Portugal (Mount Torre, 1,993 metres). I passed Andorra (Coma Pedrosa, 2,943 metres) and met two bears I scared away before heading over to the Balkans. I had to stay south and climb as many mountains as I could during the three weeks I had designated to my mountain tour. I was invited to a barbecue after climbing the highest mountain in Croatia (Dinara, 1,830 metres). I got soaking wet by the heavy rain in Serbia (Midžor, 2,169 metres). I drove past small villages with houses full of bullet holes in Bosnia (Mount Maglic, 2,386 metres). I passed big fields where battles took place. In the forest there were danger signs due to there still being mines there. But Bosnia was also one of the most beautiful places I saw during this project. I continued to Greece (Mount Olympus, 2,918 metres) where I climbed in fog. I drove past forbidden signs in Turkey (Mahya Dağı, 1,031 metres). I got attacked by a wild dog in Bulgaria (Musala, 2,925 metres).

The schedule was hectic: wake up early to drive the last hours to the next country and mountain. Climb it. Be back down by evening. Drive as far as I could to the next mountain. Try to find somewhere to sleep (that was not always so easy so sometimes I had to sleep in the car). Repeat. All I ate during these weeks were things you could buy at a gas station. That meant cookies and crisps. This diet and the lack of sleep started to make me depressed.

I was climbing the highest mountain in Romania (Moldoveanu Peak, 2,544 metres). It's remote, you need to climb six other peaks to get to the summit. It was already October and I was all alone on the mountain. I knew there were a lot of sheepdogs (these animals are very aggressive in this region and it was the thing I was most scared of during the project) and that there could be bears and wolves around. I started at lunchtime so it was sunset when I was on the summit. I had to go all the way back in the dark. Four hours later I was back at the car. I turned on the engine and the lights and a bear with two cubs was standing in front of me. My heart skipped a beat. I froze and thought how happy I was I had not met them a few minutes ago on the trail. Then I watched them move away and I backed the car and drove, shaking a little. I started to make my way to the next country: Moldova.

But the next day when I reached the border, I was not welcome. I could not pass with my rental car unless I had the original registration papers. By this point I was exhausted and stressed. I had only a few days left before I had to be back in

Italy to go on a date! I was dating an American photographer and we were planning on spending a week in the Dolomites together. At the border they told me I could park the car in Romania and take the bus over. The only problem was where I was going there were no buses. Often the mountains are remote, located in the middle of nowhere. Access with a car is almost the only way to get there if you don't have unlimited time. And I didn't. It was October and since August I had only climbed 17 mountains – and now my list had 61 mountains instead of 49.

I knew people were going to say, "Denmark's highest mountain, how difficult can that be? What about the Faroe Islands?" And I wanted to be able to say, "I did that one too." So, I added some territories. For the UK it was not only Ben Nevis on the list. It was the highest peaks in England (Scafell Pike, 978 metres), Scotland (Ben Nevis, 1,345 metres), Wales (Snowdon, 1,085 metres), Northern Ireland (Slieve Donard, 850 metres), the Isle of Man (Snaefell, 620 metres), Jersey (Les Platons, 136 metres) and Guernsey (Le Moulin, 114 metres).

It was impossible to get into Moldova, so I decided to drive to Ukraine instead. Twelve hours later (there are no highways in Romania, only small roads, so it takes a long time to get anywhere), I was at the border of Ukraine. Here I faced the same problem: I could not get into the country with my rental car. I started crying. I was so tired and depressed. I did not know what to do. I was stuck in Romania. They would not let me pass anywhere. The border police told me to go to an EU country. I looked at the map: Hungary was the closest, so I went there!

On the fourth day in Romania I reached the border with Hungary to once again face the fact that my Italian rental car was not welcome. I started to panic. I can't get out of the country! I'm stuck in Romania! Then I told myself, "You are a privileged girl from a Western country, you don't get to be upset by not being able to pass a border because if your life depended on it, you could go to the airport and fly home. Think about everyone who is escaping for their lives and can't pass. You don't get to feel sorry for yourself."

I decided to try the next possible border: Serbia. I had been to Serbia before with this car. It should work. And it did. Barely. I had to talk my way into the country at the border station because they did not want to let me in there either.

I was finally out of Romania! I felt so happy that I decided to pass through Slovenia and climb Triglav (2,864 metres) before my time was up. Triglav is a two-day climb, but I had to do it in just one day. It was a long day, but one of the most memorable climbs. It was just mind-blowingly beautiful and the weather was perfect. I met a group of Australians on the way and it was just so nice to be around people again. I had been pretty lonely over the past weeks. I decided that if I ever took on a project like this again I would do it slower to be able to enjoy it more.

As winter was coming, I moved on to lower mountains. I went to the UK and Ireland. Snowdon was amazing and beautiful. Then I got lost in the dark in the fog on Scafell Pike. And then there was one more thing.... Before deciding to climb the highest mountain in every country in Europe, I had booked to go on an expedition to climb Aconcagua (6,962 metres) in Argentina. So, within my timeline of climbing 61 mountains in a year I also had to leave for a month to climb the highest mountain in South America.

I didn't reach the top of Aconcagua on that expedition because we had a super-cold summit day. It was −40°C with wind chill and I turned around at 6,400 metres to avoid frostbite. My hands and feet were so cold.

When I got back home in January, I was tired of taking the easy way up. I wanted to develop as a climber, so I decided to do some mountains on skis. The only problem was I didn't know how to ski, so I had to learn. I spent every weekend going up north in Sweden to learn and practice. I wanted to do a winter climb, so I went to the Faroe Islands and climbed Slættaratindur (880 metres). And I did Ben Nevis via Ledge Route on a beautiful sunny winter day with Sandy Allan. He said Ben Nevis only gets about five sunny winter days a year. The next day we climbed a gully in typical Scottish winter weather with no visibility and 100 kilometre-an-hour winds.

In the beginning of April I skied the highest mountain in Norway, Galdhøpiggen. You use skins under your skis and that makes it possible to go uphill. I remember the first bit was very steep and there was a lot of ice. It was hard to keep up with the Norwegians (they are born with skis under their feet more or less). Then it became flatter and toward the end we took off the skis and walked up for the last hour to the top. Then we skied around the mountain and had to do two rappels. The weather was amazing and when we finally started to ski down it was one of the best ski days of my life. Untouched powder and not too steep.

Afterward I had so many blisters on my feet that the following week when I skied the highest mountain in Iceland, Hvannadalshnúkur (2,110 metres), I needed to use 14 Compeeds on each foot. In fact, one blister on each foot was infected and about 3 centimetres in diameter. When my glacier guide saw this he took out his pocket knife and cut them off. I wanted to scream in pain every step up to the top of Hvannadalshnúkur, but I kept it together as we were skiing down in a storm. Neither me or the glacier guide really knew how to ski. It probably looked like some kids on the first day of ski school. It wasn't beautiful, but we did it!

I started feeling stressed. I had only a few months left before my deadline at the end of July and so many mountains to climb. A planned photography tour in Patagonia for a few weeks and then ten days of climbing four 5,000-metre mountains in Peru wasn't the best idea, but it was planned before I had taken on this project. I came home a month later and it was mid-May. Finally, the climbing season was about to start!

I climbed cool ridges in Slovakia (Gerlachovský štít, 2,654 metres). I went to Azerbaijan (Mount Bazarduzu, 4,466 metres) and South Ossetia (Mount Khalatsa, 3,938 metres). Back to Ukraine (Mount Hoverla, 2,061 metres) and Moldova (Bălănești Hill, 430 metres). I sneaked in to Transnistria (Transnistria high point, 273 metres). I had a month left and nine mountains still to climb: all of the mountains in the Alps, four more in the Balkans and Finland and Sweden to climb.

I ran up Zugspitze (2,962 metres) in Germany to beat a thunderstorm. In Austria, instead of taking the "easy" route, I climbed the Stüdlgrat ridge on Grossglockner (3,798 metres). It was my favourite of the whole project because I climbed a technical ridge to the top and it was just within my limit. I had to balance on razor-thin ridges and climb over big blocks. It was scary, but still possible and helped me develop as a climber. I really enjoyed the technical part of it. The guide, Peter, was amazing – he let me be independent and did not drag me to the top. I felt badass doing that climb. It was much more fun and challenging than the normal way up. After that I went for Monte Rosa Dufourspitze (4,634 metres) in Switzerland. The hardest mountain in the whole project (if you only climb via normal routes). I had a lot of respect for this mountain. I had read about other people trying to complete this project and break the world record, but who did not succeed because they could not climb Dufourspitze. I had been waiting a long time for a good-weather window, so when it finally came of course all guides were fully booked. I tried to get an experienced partner to come with me, but it turns out none of my Facebook contacts climb mountains. The only one I could talk into coming was a guy I met on Tinder a few months earlier. He was from Costa Rica, living in Stockholm. He was a sport climber, but he had never seen snow, or used crampons or an ice axe. He said he would join me and I was desperate so it was the best I could do.

This meant that I had to put all the experience I had gathered during the year to the test. I had to lead this climb. We hiked halfway to the Monte Rosa Hut. We scouted the route and acclimatized. We opted for an alpine start and, since we knew the way, all the guides were following me. We navigated through crevasses. The sun came up. We crossed the glacier. We climbed the ridge. And we reached the top of the highest mountain in Switzerland after 6 hours. Then we had to run down and with 1 minute to spare we caught the last train down to Zermatt.

My friend from Costa Rica joined me in the Balkans. We got turned around by a storm in Montenegro. Hiked to the top of the highest mountain in Albania, Mount Korab (2,764 metres). And got a local hunter to join us up to the top of Rudoka (2,658 metres) in Kosovo. They don't really know what mountain is the highest there so I climbed another just in case, called Đeravica (2,656 metres). And standing on the top of Đeravica I cried.

Because now I knew I could make it. I had a little bit more than one week left and only two more mountains to climb.

I started driving from Kosovo to Halti (1,325 metres) in northern Finland. The drive took a while. The climb was done in a few hours and I started feeling really excited. I had saved the highest mountain in Sweden (Kebnekaise, 2,098 metres) for last. As the grand finale. And I got this stupid idea to climb it in a superhero suit. Because that is how I felt.

I put my whole life on hold for a year to do this crazy mountain project. I was just a regular girl. Not a professional athlete. I had almost no experience. I didn't really have time for it. No money. But I had to do this.

So, four days before the year was up, I stood on top of the last mountain with a 4-metre-long cape blowing in the wind and as I traversed from the northern summit to the south it felt pretty epic. I had made it!

Or at least that's what I thought. But when I came back down, "100 Country High Points" – a guy who had also climbed the highest mountains in countries all over the world – had sent me a text: "You went up on the wrong hill in Luxembourg."

I could not believe it! I had to hurry to Luxembourg to go up the right hill. The highest point is about 300 metres and it's marked by a rock next to the road. The one I went up is about 300 metres away, but I was thankful he had told me about this.

It had been 363 days since I stood on top of Mount Elbrus in Russia and I had climbed 61 mountains, as well as the extra ones in South America. Not too bad.

What *was* really bad after all of this was my finances. Over the year I had worked as a photographer when I was not out climbing mountains. And when I went climbing I always did a couple of mountains per trip. So I had no social life at all for a year – I was only focusing on work and climbing. But the work I did wasn't enough. A couple of months after it was over, business was not going well and I was broke. I came to the conclusion that the only option was to sell my apartment to get money to pay my employees' salaries and fill the hole in my bank account.

Despite all of this, I realized that this experience had been the greatest thing I had ever done in my life; and not only that – it totally changed it, too. It was impossible to go back to a normal life again. It made me reflect on my life, the way I live it and what's important to me. And I realized that I'm living my dream. I don't want to change anything. I love the mountains and I would die if I did not climb them.

ORDINARY THINGS WITH EXTRAORDINARY PEOPLE

EWA KALISIEWICZ

Ewa Kalisiewicz, born in 1986 in Warsaw, Poland, is an active life and outdoors enthusiast. She's an accomplished skydiver and BASE jumper with wingsuit flying as her favourite discipline. Ewa (with her team of three) was awarded first place at the sixth International Artistic Wingsuit Competition and was also declared the best performing wingsuit camera flyer in 2013. With over 1,200 skydives and over 800 BASE jumps, she combines wingsuit flying with climbing and mountaineering. Ewa is also a wingsuit flying coach. She lives in Switzerland with her husband, Tim Howell, a pro mountaineer, skier, BASE jumper and a wingsuit pilot who inspires and motivates her to set new goals and work toward their completion regardless of how long the process will be.

Ewa graduated from Aviation Management at the National Defence University of Warsaw and has worked with the International Air Transport Association (IATA) since 2010, currently managing industry payment projects.

Find out more about Ewa at:

@ewakalisiewicz

Jumping out of perfectly fine aircrafts. Hopping off randomly found bridges and cliffs during a road trip on the coast. Preparing for and executing a stunning climb in the Italian Aosta Valley and flying back down in a wingsuit, carrying the rope and hardware underneath it. All that while having a full-time office job – absolutely normal. Let me tell you my story, a story of an ordinary year with highlights, as the seasons change, of activities that make me feel accomplished and happy and, most importantly, bring me closer to wonderful people who are not afraid to live their lives to the fullest. I tend to say I'm doing ordinary things with extraordinary people – my husband, my friends – who share the same definition of "normal". It is tough, at times, to combine professional and family life with adventures. I've learned that planning and time management, combined with self-discipline for execution, lay the perfect foundation for a well-balanced and happy life.

Winter

Who doesn't list their new year's resolutions? I do, in the form of a recap of the past year and a to-do list for the coming months. Although wingsuit flying is my favourite discipline, I don't practise it much during winter. Skiing, ski touring and mountaineering take priority. As I live in close proximity to the Alps, skiing is a natural choice for this time of the year. However, as I was born and raised in Warsaw, Poland, I knew skiing would be a great challenge, but I'd never thought it would also bring so much joy! I had skied only occasionally as a teenager, participating in a mandatory winter-school camp hosted in a village in low-rising hills in Tatra County. I most definitely did not enjoy skiing back then – I felt clumsy and misplaced. Only at the age of 30, having moved to Switzerland, did I rediscover what the snowy mountains have to offer, especially in a backcountry setting, far away from the piste and ski lifts, with very few people around. This is where I feel free – in these silent, magnificent surroundings, where nature makes you remember how small you really are.

It took many days of ski practice before I attempted my first off-piste skiing in Vallée Blanche, Chamonix, which can be described simply as a fantastic journey into the largest glaciated domain in the Alps, the Mont Blanc massif. It was a mind-blowing 20-kilometre-long, off-piste route with a vertical descent of 2,700 metres. My first descent was not life-threatening, but I didn't feel fully comfortable there yet, as it's riddled with crevasses and there can be a high risk of ice-cliff collapse and avalanches. Also, the fresh snow makes it more difficult to get through, unless you're an experienced powder skier. Once I had completed more training with Tim, my husband, who is an excellent skier, all of the next off-piste adventures felt much more enjoyable. I had a better awareness of my surroundings, enjoying fully the wilderness of the winter wonderland.

This is when I also started climbing the 4,000-metre peaks of the Alps on skis. Certain routes on these mountains are more enjoyable to ascend and descend with the use of skis. Winter isn't the normal mountaineering season, with the shorter daylight hours, adverse climbing conditions with harsher temperatures and winds. But I had my sights set on completing another 4,000-metre mountain in the Alps: Allalinhorn, 4,027 metres, a relatively easy climb with a ski descent of over 2,000 metres all the way back to the valley floor. Tim and I summited in good time even with the icy summit. The lack of snow and high winds had stripped this slope of frozen snow to reveal instead black ice, which made it impossible to ski over. The descent was where it all went wrong. As I was kicking in steps with my crampon, an attachment point snapped. Using my axe to lessen the fall, I held my weight on the pick, now dug into the ice. Tim was above, holding the rope attached to me, anchoring himself into the snow as a dead weight. It was now a slow and delicate process to get down this ice slope safely. I secured myself with an ice screw while Tim put me on the belay, so that I could confidently climb down to our ski cache. I was happy to have my reliable skis back on instead of malfunctioning crampons. My calves were burning after this tense situation, but luckily at this stage there were "only" 2,000 metres of ski descent to conclude the mission down to Saas Fee.

Situations like these are often called "type two fun". In the moment it's not fun – it's scary and potentially dangerous – but I look back and enjoy it through hindsight. I know we had the situation under control. In that moment, filled with uncertainty, we have to adapt. In these times it's even more important to stay rational and calm while resolving the situation. The scarier it was in that moment, the more I enjoy looking back at it with satisfaction. I sat in the car and grinned from ear to ear, then realized I had to go back to work tomorrow.

Spring

Spring heralds the start of wingsuit flying season. After spending over eight years wingsuit flying, I find it is not hard to get back into it after the winter break. I wouldn't say it's as simple as riding a bicycle, but having completed over 800 flights, the body builds up muscle memory and habits that, if learned properly, are certainly quite natural to refresh. Spring kicks off with continuous training for the more demanding and less forgiving spots to fly. The long ascent often combines climbing and mountaineering, with ropes, crampons and axes, and is celebrated with, in comparison, a short 2-minute flight back down.

One of the most memorable ones was climbing Aiguille Croux (3,256 metres) on the Italian side of Mont Blanc, in the Aosta Valley. The conditions that weekend looked promising, so having shut down my computer at the Geneva office, that Friday evening we drove straight to the bottom of the mountain. There we left the car near the place where, the next morning, we would land our parachutes. The final bag check revealed we had packed everything: wingsuit, parachute and helmet, the rope, harness, belay device and some carabiners. The mountaineering boots on our feet would serve for the climb the next morning. Our alpine attire was already on and our snack bars would accommodate for dinner and breakfast. There was no room for any extra weight bearing in mind that we would be flying back down with everything we were taking or using it to get up to the summit.

The first part was to cover a 2-hour via ferrata, making our way to the refuge for the night. As the sun quickly disappeared over the horizon, Tim and I made the most of the hike with the head torches on, lighting the path ahead. The hut was quiet, normally hosting up to 50 people; only our four companions greeted us upon arrival. In the morning, after having a quick bite, we started the hike to the bottom of the climb and divided into two teams of three. The climb itself was not the fastest one, but that only meant that we had the joy of sharing more time on the mountain together. We were not in a hurry that morning; the weather was just perfect, with close to zero winds and beautiful blue skies above us forecasting excellent flying conditions. Having reached the top around midday, we allowed ourselves a few minutes of relaxing in the sun, like lizards enjoying sunrays.

Wingsuit flying is without a doubt my favourite part of every mountain ascent of this kind. I see it as a pure human flight, free of any solid structure or machinery. The modern wingsuit, improved with years of research, development and testing, is nothing more than stitched pieces of airtight fabric. The jump preparation itself is like a ritual: each BASE jumper has their own sequence of checks and gearing-up routine. This was also when we placed the climbing gear either on the harness underneath the wingsuit or in its inside pockets, with the rope wrapped around the waist. We had decided to fly in pairs, me teaming up with Tim as we know each other's exits and flights perfectly – executing the flight as per the usual routine gives me peace of mind on a new jumping site. I counted from three backward... three, two, one... and pushed off a solid rocky ledge of Aiguille Croux into the void. The moment of the exit is remarkable: total silence, around and inside you. There are no other thoughts than deep focus as you're bound to execute the plan you've put together. As I accelerated, the air rushed through the inlets in my wingsuit, pressurizing the internal cells. The suit now acted as an aerofoil, giving me the ability to glide, dive and turn at speeds of 200 kilometres per hour, first past the glacier below me, then the ridge below that, following its line until the grassy landing came into sight. I was flying with good speed; here, speed is your friend. The visual references and instinct were telling me it was time to deploy my parachute. I increased my glide, increasing my vertical distance away from the rocky surroundings, and reached back to pull my pilot chute. This small circular parachute acts as a drogue and in turn pulls out the main parachute. As I approached landing on a green grassy stretch, I couldn't help the feeling of accomplishment – the years of flying and time spent climbing came together on that glorious morning, truly combining both together.

Summer

Summer is the best time for "ticking off" wingsuit exit points in new locations: the days are long, the weather is warm, the winter snow has long melted, so there are fewer obstacles to accessing those places. But it's also the best time for certain mountaineering routes. This summer I climbed a few 4,000-metre peaks in the Alps, including the classic Mont Blanc via the three mounts route. Even though I don't specifically remember preparing for it, I believe it was when all the endurance and climbing preparation came in handy. Tim and I, accompanied by another pair of climbers, started the summit attempt from Aiguille du Midi, which we had trekked to on a Saturday evening. The mountain hut there, where we stayed overnight, was a very basic, old winter hut, the draughty door allowing the cold air inside. Fatigued mattresses on shaky wooden bunk beds just added to the atmosphere of adventure! Having to provide your own sleeping arrangements, as well as meals, makes the experience even more remarkable when you're self-sufficient.

That night, spent at an altitude of 3,800 metres, was our chance to acclimatize, as by noon the next day we aimed to be standing on the summit of Mont Blanc. My fellow companions would call it an "alpine start", whereas I still call getting up at 3 a.m. a brutal disruptor to beauty sleep. We were ready to go within 20 minutes of waking up and the ascent began in a pitch-black darkness. We found the route to be slightly out of condition; the crevasses are covered by compacted snow that you hope don't collapse. Surprisingly, the thought of turning back didn't even cross my mind. That just made the climb even more interesting. Our first efforts were rewarded by the simple pleasure of watching the sunrise over the stunning Mont Blanc massif.

As the climb progressed, one of the team members began to suffer from altitude sickness and decided to turn around, together with her partner. Which left me and Tim continuing alone. How lucky we are that rapid altitude gain doesn't impact us, I'm tempted to say! The previous winter we had climbed Mount Kenya, reaching 4,500 metres altitude in one go, starting at sea level. Mont Blanc was just slightly higher, but we had spent the night at altitude already. I remember well our sunburned lips in the absence of chapstick, our freezing cheeks due to the crazy winds and our cold hands regardless of our warm mittens. The route to the summit was long, broken with interesting sections where we had to use both axes and crampons to dig into an almost vertical wall. That's how I imagine ice climbing. I hadn't expected that along our route. The views from the summit were stunning, especially to the Italian side, where we could spot the cliff we flew our wingsuits from some days before.

To alternate the descent, we chose a different route that led us all the way back down to Les Houches, making it approximately 15 hours of continuous effort. It was just another adventure that was fitted in around my busy work schedule that, most of the time, only guaranteed free weekends. Therefore, most of the climbs had to be, and were, accomplished just using the weekend break. As with the example of the Mont Blanc climb, we set off on Saturday and concluded on Sunday; by the evening we were back home and preparing for the busy working week on Monday morning.

Autumn

Autumn is definitely my favourite time of year. The experiences of the first three quarters of the year make me feel fit, capable and energized. The season brings the simple pleasures of long hikes, camping, flying with a wingsuit above the beautifully coloured alpine trees. Being surrounded by great adventure enthusiasts and pro athletes, I find some of them naturally gifted toward certain disciplines. There are those who put on a wingsuit and show the signs of natural ease at flying from the first try. Others become solid climbers within months, scaling up the grade ladder almost effortlessly. Honestly, I am not one of those. It took me years of dedication, training and patience to achieve progress in all the sports I practise. My professional life is important to me. It presents a different kind of challenge, which I also enjoy. But I strive to make the most of my time out of the office. I may not remember what kept me working late last year, but I surely will remember the time when, after an exhausting climb on Aiguille du Moine, I passed by the refuge on the way down and managed to... put on somebody else's boots and walk them back down to Chamonix! I was commenting, along the route, how happy I was with them and how comfortably they fit me. What a shame that I had to return them the same day.

Seeking an escape to a hot, sunny place a few years ago, we planned a trip to South Africa. We spent only a couple of days at each location as we drove down the coast from Kruger National Park. Toward the end, in Cape Town, we could absorb our surroundings a bit more as we had five days left before flying home. While we waited for the winds to die down, we spent a few days at the usual tourist sites as well as climbing the arrow arête route of Table Mountain, which follows a line directly under the cable car. On the penultimate day the winds looked good and we aimed to make the most of it. Our intention was to wingsuit fly from Table Mountain, looking out to the coast and then land in a rugby field, which the owner kindly allows as a landing zone. As we put our suits and parachutes on, getting ready for the jump, Tim went down on one knee and proposed. I wasn't expecting that at all – at least, the time and place was a surprise. It's only now when I reflect on that moment that I realize I have never seen him nervous like that before or after. His voice wavered. He was nervous, way more so than on any BASE jump he had ever done. I said yes with glee, and a ripple of applause erupted. Unbeknown to us, a crowd could see us from a viewing deck about 50 metres behind us.

We did our final gear checks and pushed off the cliff, flying together. There was a slight coastal wind and, combined with our attempt to fly together, it limited our performance. We both pulled our parachutes before the rugby field. My parachute opened slowly, the lines twisting as it pressurized. A nuisance more than a malfunction, but it would mean I couldn't make the primary landing area. I took a downwind landing, which just added speed to my landing in an area of shrubland. I hit something with my lower leg, which made me fall painfully to the ground. Sitting up, trying to reconcile what had just happened, I noticed there was a clean cut on my wingsuit, halfway between the knee and the foot. I made sure I could bend my knee and wiggle my toes – meaning my leg was still attached and somehow functioning, yet I was too scared to unzip the wingsuit to take a look at the inevitable damage. This was when Tim came rushing up to me, and as he unzipped my wingsuit I looked back up to where we had jumped from.

My leg was bandaged with an improvised dressing, and Tim was certain I shouldn't be walking on it. It wasn't bleeding enough for blood loss to be a concern and I was sure we could make it to the car without needing assistance. Tim would fireman-carry me a hundred metres or so before going back to get our bags. While he was carrying the equipment, I would walk the remaining insignificant distance, trying to progress as much as possible – much to Tim's dismay as I didn't know how bad the injury was. We repeated this process for 2 hours before we reached the car and could make it to the hospital. Only when the makeshift bandages were cut off did the nurses realize how bad the injury was. I had hit a tree stump. A dagger-like edge cut through the wingsuit and de-gloved my shin; the bone was clearly visible and fortunately clearly intact. Tim took some photos to show me later, but I made a point of not wanting to see the injury until I was back flying. I intended to be back flying as soon as possible and didn't want any mental associations to put me off.

The wound healed, the scars are still obvious, but I was back flying three months after the incident. It was still my favourite trip for so many reasons, and that was a day I'll never forget, also for many reasons! One of them being that Tim lost the engagement ring during all the commotion while my leg was being put back together by a plastic surgeon.

TUMPING
AND TRIPPING
HANNAH MAIA

Hannah Maia is an award-winning filmmaker based in the Lake District, England, where she runs a small production company called Maia Media. After graduating in visual anthropology and ethnographic filmmaking, Hannah began to teach herself to make films and tell stories. Her most recent film, *My Big White Thighs & Me*, is a personal story which encourages us all to turn down the volume on the demands of the world and to celebrate the quiet heroism of a female life and her body. It is a story about womanhood, miscarriage, healing, loving your own skin and freezing your bum off in cold water. Hannah is currently working on a documentary about women canoeing in the Canadian wilderness called *Wood On Water*, to be released in summer 2020. She's also a passionate mountain biker and outdoor swimmer.

Find out more about Hannah at:
I/F: @maiamedia

Muskeg is a delight unknown to many and it's not easy to identify. Step in it and it creates a farting noise, then engulfs your leg. If you're lucky you will only sink up to your ankle; but oftentimes much more of you goes in. It consumes shoes, it rips off socks and sometimes you need help to get out. It's a dark tar-like substance probably with a lot of beaver poop in it. I don't know what the exact botanical definition is, but essentially muskeg is a floating peat bog. It's sphagnum moss and a lot of decaying vegetation. It's a large thing of mud that's stinky and out here in the taiga of northern Quebec I'm surrounded by it. The coniferous forests of this subarctic region are criss-crossed with thousands of lakes, rivers and swamps, and the ground can appear wet and spongy but often it conceals sinkholes, which makes walking arduous and a little dangerous.

Right now, I'm in a canoe, so I'm safe from muskeg for the time being. I'm paddling the Eastmain River with 11 women and ahead of us are seemingly endless white-tipped choppy waves. My hood is cinched tight as rain drips from my nose. Relentless headwinds rock and roll our small wood-and-canvas vessel while the gunnels sit low in the water due to our heavy load. Despite the fact that we are paddling down river, the winds are so strong that if we stop paddling for even seconds, we are pushed back upstream.

I am bowman, sitting in the front of the canoe, and though one of my responsibilities is to keep a look out for hidden rocks under the surface of the water, I find myself occasionally allowing my wind-stung eyes to rest closed. My paddle strokes barely falter and I sway from the hips collecting micro-sleeps. Repetitive and trance-like, in that moment I realize it's one of the first times I can't hear anyone sing.

This is an epic adventure, 40 days in the northern reaches of Quebec, travelling with traditional tools like wood-canvas canoes and fire irons to enable cooking over an open fire. It is a trip filled with unknowns for me, but there is one thing of which I'm sure: the 11 young women I'm travelling with, nine of whom are teenagers, will not see each other at their best. Think bug-bitten, cold and boob-deep in muskeg bog while carrying an incredibly heavy canoe on their heads.

My primary role on this trip is as an independent filmmaker, but I can't escape the fact that the work of tripping often consumes my efforts and energies. Carrying my own load, paddling, keeping pace with the group, constantly on the go, means inevitably shots will suffer, both technically and aesthetically. The magic of a brief wolf sighting... missed, as I struggled to put down my paddle and grab my camera. But balancing this is my hope that on-the-ground intimacy will prove rewarding in a way that brings alive the trip, and enhances my understanding and ability to shape the story.

I asked myself numerous times on this trip, how did I get here? And like most of life's grand adventures, the seeds of it were planted many moons ago. I'd recently finished a film about the size of my thighs, swimming in cold water and learning to love my skin again, and I was looking for another creative project. I wrote down a list of things that were important to me:

1. Water. I love water.
2. I love stories about real women's lives. I think it's good to use my voice as a woman to tell stories about other women.
3. A general passion and respect for wilderness, adventure and just being outside.

Again and again, for me, the creative process has shown itself to be bigger than I am. As I clarified my own interests around "what's next", I received an email out of the blue from a stranger in America. Having never met me before, Maxine had just seen my most recent film and wanted to tell me about young women doing hard things in a magical and remote region of Quebec. And so began a conversation where I was introduced to things I'd never heard of before and which began to shape a most wondrous picture in my mind. A place where "pocket bacon" and "goo balls" existed, where you would find slippy "monster rocks" and "birthday trees". A place that could send you utterly "bush honkers" crazy or set your soul on fire. Needless to say, I was intrigued...

As I delved into this story, I was fascinated to find out that a group of teenage girls would gather together at the start of every summer on a small island in Canada. Over six weeks of summer, this all-girl group paddle traditional wood-canvas canoes through the remote northern wilderness, travelling a network of streams, lakes, rivers, mudholes and muskeg bogs, with one resupply via float plane. Ultimately their sights are set on Hudson Bay.

I was captivated from the get-go, simultaneously wondering what kind of teenage girl would really want to forego all of life's luxuries and spend their summer in the wilderness – and yet knowing as a teenager I probably would have been one of them.

Fast-forward to the present and I am one of them. I'm also more than twice their age, hurtling toward 40, with the youngest of the nine girls only 15. Youthful shrieks, goofiness and the boundless energy of the teenage girls I'm travelling with are a constant reminder that I am – relatively – old. I hear them quietly talking about my loud snoring and I want to tell them, "I didn't snore when I was 16 you know," but I'm wise enough to know better.

I also feel different because I'm a mum now with a toddler waiting for me at home and my body is oh-so different, too. Joints ache, creek and swell. Whereas these teenage bodies seem to rebound from precarious twists and tumbles over rocks and tree roots, I'm acutely aware that a twisted knee on a portage trail (an overland trail where we carry our canoes and gear to link together lakes or avoid an obstacle in a river) might provide lingering pain for months, not just a day or two. I'm therefore careful, considered and cautious; while my pride insists I not be the slow or weak link of the expedition. I'm different from these girls and yet the same.

At the heart of this story is an American summer camp – but not as most people know it. The camp is called Keewaydin and it's the oldest operating summer camp in North America. It's steeped in history and operates with the same vision as when it was established in 1893, which is to offer "a programme focused on wilderness canoe tripping, with minimum time spent in base camp". For the first 105 years it was only boys that had the chance to go tripping, but in the past 20 years girls have joined the ranks and now take on their own all-girl trips. I'm interested in how something established over a century ago to promote manliness and "roughing it in the woods" can still be relevant for teenage girls today.

As a filmmaker, I'm keenly aware that I'm asking a lot from these teenagers to allow me to be here with them and film this very vulnerable experience they have out here in the woods. I want to try and honour that as much as possible, to ensure that it still feels like their trip and a safe space for them to be themselves.

The style of tripping is counter-cultural, its essence slow and purposeful. The group equipment is the same style of gear as that used over a hundred years ago. We cook on open wood fires and the loads we carry are canvas duffel bags and wannigans – large, sturdy traditional wooden boxes. Gear is portaged using tumplines – a leather strap positioned on top of the head aligning the weight down the spine rather than on shoulder straps. And we paddle in beautiful wood-canvas canoes following routes that are centuries old.

When you first put a heavily loaded wannigan on your head using a leather tumpline, it's uncomfortable. Awkward. Definitely painful. Freshly loaded it could easily weigh 35 kilograms, add a large daypack or a tent on top and you're looking at much more. With practice you perfect your tump and gradually it becomes easier. Dare I say, it even begins to feel comforting. A slow, steady and grounding weight in which you can take pride in yourself for hauling. On a long portage you learn to not put the load down because any rest gained is lost in the effort to pick it back up again.

I don't think it's an overstatement to say Canada was born on the back of a canoe. The First Nations people built birch-bark canoes and then showed the non-indigenous people who came over how to travel in them. Birch-bark canoes were in turn used as the template for the wood-canvas canoes developed in the nineteenth century when demand for boats outstripped the supply of birch bark.

Demand for canoes became so high because in 1670 King Charles II of England signed a Royal Charter that governed trading rights in the Hudson Bay watershed. The charter served as the original articles of incorporation of the Hudson's Bay Company and stated that the company was to control all lands whose rivers and streams drain into Hudson Bay – an area comprising more than 1.5 million square miles, approximately 40 per cent of modern-day Canada. Of course, it's a dubious claim that the King of England's signature on a piece of parchment in 1670 could effectively bestow sovereignty over such a vast land and ignore the indigenous people who already possessed and occupied that land. Regardless, the charter did lead to the establishment of large outposts where pelts and furs were traded.

Consequently, much of the story of Canada's fur trade unfolded along the country's many great waterways, with canoes as the dominant transportation carrying goods and fur to the trading ports of Hudson Bay. Indigenous hunters, early explorers and voyageurs tirelessly paddled their canoes in search of furs, which led to the mapping of the interior lakes and rivers of Canada.

It's on these trails and transportation routes developed by the necessity to trade that we travel today. As we paddle the majestic Eastmain River we're in indigenous Cree territory and as our experiences mesh with theirs the route is kept open. When searching for a portage we look for a blaze on a tree made with a single axe cut or even strips of a bandana marking the path.

Having spent the past 10 hours paddling, lumbering and lumping our canoes and gear, we are beat. At the start of a dank and buggy portage we have decided to bushwhack our own campsite and I have found a hummock with a spot just big enough to fit my tent lengthways between two large mossy rocks. As I pitch my tent, I wonder what the point of it all is. Where was all the fun? Why were these teenagers here? Then through the bushes I hear one of the girls exclaim "It's perfect!" and in that moment I realize two things. Firstly, the camp spot they have just found is anything but perfect. And secondly, it's all about perspective. I really admire these girls for their cheerful optimism and their non-stop singing. I also realize I am hungry.

A trip like this strengthens your resilience. I'm surrounded by bugs that bite, sting and annoy. I've come to realize that mosquitoes and blackfly are some of the real guardians of the Canadian wilderness and when I'm wet and cold the bugs are that extra little thing that nearly send me over the edge.

On several days we wake at 5 a.m. and don't get to the next campsite until 8 p.m. that night still with several hours of chores to do – chop wood, erect the fly, make dinner, bake bannock (a type of bread inherited from early settlers and fur traders) for tomorrow's lunch, put up tents, wash pots and dishes... sleep. Slowly, as the trip progresses, I witness the girls finding joy in the simple day-to-day tasks. They laugh full-heartedly and sing as they scrub endlessly at the pot-black on the bottom of the pans.

One day mid-paddle a seminal moment takes place when I take my bra off. It was deemed surplus to requirements. Not needed. No thank you. Adios chafing! Slowly, I realize I'm beginning to feel comfortable with being uncomfortable. I'm not resisting any more. I'm finding my groove. Despite the tireless hard work I begin to enjoy canoe travel and the rhythm of life on water. From the seat of my canoe I am often fully immersed in introspective feelings, which leads to a lightness on my shoulders and an ebbing of my woes. We're finding our rhythm, as days follow a pattern. Life becomes simple and fundamentally essential.

I watch in awe as young women carry heavy loads down mini rock cliffs. But the best bit is witnessing the fun, laughter and lightness that occurs when women get together far from the stresses of everyday life. It's empowering to be surrounded by women all proud and happy to be using their body for strength. To be sweaty and dirty is expected.

This is not a trip fuelled by adrenaline – although padding large rapids in a wooden boat and catching a 3-foot pike do provide that occasionally. It's really about appreciating the slow purposefulness of wilderness travel. When I'm on the water there's a sense of peace that is almost spiritual, and when portaging there's a huge potential for personal growth through resilience and struggle.

There are easier ways to canoe trip. Sending your child off in a hand-built wood-canvas canoe, with wooden boxes filled with heavy tin cans just as they did over 100 years ago, could seem a little contrived. But if you're going to travel on lakes and rivers, through vast landscapes and be among the quiet and the weather and all of it... why not give yourself time to be in that space. If our only goal is to go from A to B as fast and easily as possible, then perhaps some value is lost.

I enjoy my time unplugged and in the wilderness – my chance to tap into that elusive something that seems to be missing from our modern lives. And I'm proud to be part of a small club of people who not only know what muskeg is but have been stuck knee deep in it.

———

Back home after a trip like this creativity zips through my veins as I grapple with my creative ideas for the film and ultimately muster the courage to share it with the world.

Finding our voice and sharing it; telling stories, exciting and empowering others is a powerful motivator. Right now from the depths of my editing cave this sentiment from writer and poet Kate Tempest resonates completely:

> You've gone through the agony of taking an idea that is perfect – it's soaring, it comes from this other place – then you've had to summon it down and process it through your shit brain. It's coming out of your shit hands and you've ruined it completely. The finished thing is never going to be anywhere near as perfect as the idea, of course, because if it was, why would you ever do anything else?

Of course, then we have another idea and invest ourselves in a whole new project. And each of these finished things act as stepping stones toward being able to find our voice – be that as a teenager, an adventurer, a woman or a storyteller.

I suppose all of it comes down to resilience.

THE GREAT DIVIDE

JENN HILL

Jenn Hill was a rider and writer. She inspired many with her quiet, thoughtful tales of cycling. When racing, she was the one who smiled and said hello while lapping you, but was overcome with shyness on the podium. Always modest about her own achievements, in 2008 Jenn set off across the Atlantic to take part in the Great Divide race, down the spine of the American Rocky Mountains. She finished 2,400 miles away at the Mexican border a mere 22 days later. On a singlespeed. She was diagnosed with terminal lung cancer in 2014, and died the following year. She continued riding until little more than a month before her death. Always with a smile on her face. This story was originally told in *Singletrack* magazine.

eaving Del Norte under cover of darkness, we spin out of the desert toward the mountains. Cacti and sagebrush give way to pines, packed dirt to loose gravel, and we start to climb as the sky reddens behind us and the horizon resolves into morning.

The gradient is harsh and my legs refuse to wake. The strip of grey rubble breaks what little determination has crept back into the reserves overnight. I walk stretches where the steepness increases the hurt beyond what is sustainable. Start riding again when the walking twists my calves into coils of tight wire.

On and on it goes, for hours. There is nothing in the UK that can prepare you for a climb this intense. No number of interminable road drags into blasting coastal headwinds, no quantity of impossibly steep hills failed and failed and finally conquered as the strength grows in painfully small increments. Switch your brain off; let the hurt go as easily as it comes. Resistance is futile. Crest the hundredth false summit and catch your breath, look around in disbelief as gravity grabs hold of your wheels and starts to turn them without effort. You're standing on the roof of America and there's nothing left to climb.

Brake. Feet down. The silence comes barrelling over the mountains in waves. Lean on the bars for a moment, blood pounding in my ears. Raise my head and stare at the snow patches still clinging to the alpine meadow, silver grass and muddied meltwater reflecting the light of the sun. This is the high point, 11,910 feet up in the sky, and it's all downhill from here to Mexico.

I fly out of Gatwick with a bike bag and a CamelBak to my name. I have a return ticket tucked into my passport but am not sure the same girl will be coming back. Goodbyes are difficult and painful, flooded with tears that have little to do with what is to come and everything to do with what drove me on this crazy journey in the first place. The departure lounge is a welcome refuge of anonymity and quiet phone calls, and as the flight banks over the Downs and the sea I watch the trails I've called home for the past ten years disappear behind the clouds.

Calgary is a quiet city, full of cranes and half-built skyscrapers going up rapidly in the gap between winters. It rains often and much time is spent staring out of coffee shop windows, chatting to baristas, watching dipped umbrellas crossing the streets. Nobody has heard of the race and, by the time I leave, the whole endeavour feels unreal until the moment I crest a rise on the edge of the flatlands and see the Rockies, snow-capped and stretching all the way across a distant horizon. They are bigger than anything I have seen in my entire life. Awe, fear and excitement slam home and I fly down the road, feet up and grinning, crying and laughing at the same time.

I ride my bike from Calgary to Banff and then on to the border as a prologue of sorts, breaking myself in gently with five days of calm between the twin storms of end and beginning. The route proper slices five states, winding down the spine of the continent and not necessarily following the path of least resistance. When I get home in November I'll find that my father has pinned a map of the USA from ceiling to floor and traced as best he could the trail as we rode it: the scale is shocking and I have trouble reconciling it with my experience, gaps between dots bearing no relation to my experience. I'm glad I didn't do the same before I left as I would never have got on to the plane. Two thousand, four hundred and ninety-five miles is blinding if looked at as a whole. Instead, I take one day at a time and every hour as it comes. If I am tired, then I rest; if I am flying, then I ride. I have no plan, no schedule, and am very much making it up as I go along, because it's the only way I know how.

The border crossing is searches and signatures and a guard who tells me what I'm doing is dangerous and stupid. I don't mention the Kananaskis wilderness I rode through a few days before, where the trees bore claw scars eight feet above the ground and a local hunter pointed out the locations of the grizzly dens I had ridden past on my way down the deserted valley. He asks if I have bear spray and tells me I should have a gun as well. For the people, not the wildlife. I draw breath to explain why I shouldn't, then think better of it and roll away into the land of the free.

In Whitefish, Montana, it's easy to find the riders. The first and only motel in town has several loaded bikes leaning against its bright white walls, doors open, cyclists' legs stretched across beds inside. Quiet hellos are exchanged and slow conversations unfold. I realize that I belong here with these people, a world away from the forced bravado and ego puff of the UK's

24-hour race scene. They are gentle and humble and share the anticipation of what we're taking on. Mutual respect is a given and for the first time in months nobody asks me what I am doing or why I am here, just accepts that I am.

Come race day I wave goodbye to backs I may never see again. But even though the Divide is long, the disparity in daily mileage is not that great and as energy and ability ebb and flow between us, it's common to roll through a town and see familiar bikes leaning against walls, sunburned grins flashing behind massive vats of Coke. I spend entire days catching riders on a climb, being passed by them on the descent and then repeating the process a few miles down the road. Occasionally we ride together for longer stretches, chatting about the race and our homes, dreams and ideas, pasts and futures. Sometimes we share motel rooms and curse each other's snoring, waking to a flurry of activity as everybody tries not to be the last to get up and away. Pride counts, even when you've worn holes in your shorts and are reduced to fishing old peanuts out of the pocket fluff to get you to the next town. Wandering through Kremmling feeling faintly desperate, I bump into Geoff. Unsmiling and wasted, he leads me to a bar around the corner and we share a quiet supper as he tells me he is quitting the race. I know that the decision is his alone and that nothing I can say will make him feel any better, so I sip my Coke in silence and try not to think too hard about why quitting hasn't even occurred to me yet.

As the miles roll on it becomes clear that I might just make it. Every day has its own character and covering vast distances means I often see the sun set on a wholly different place to where I was when it rose. Montana is mind-blowingly beautiful yet filled with a sense of the everyday; we pass houses and farmsteads where people raise their cattle and drive their kids to school, making the splendour feel mundane. Idaho is brief and tarnished with the trappings of ski resorts and the money they bring; Colorado is mostly steep and very lonely, despite the increased contact with civilization that begins and ends with its borders. Southern New Mexico is a land of straight roads and big skies.

Fewer mountains, slower-moving time.

Wyoming is unremarkable and dominated by "the Basin" that occupies my thoughts in the preceding days and erases them entirely while trapped in its hundred-mile vortex of aimless directions and incessantly acrid wind. Escape comes in the form of an absolutely straight road with expansion joints every ten metres. Bump, bump, bump. I start to count them but the horizon never comes closer and darkness is chasing hard from behind. As the sun goes down I'm riding the banked asphalt velodrome of the Mineral X Road, lights on the interstate glittering silently distant, fire melting into chocolate black. Massive hares flank me through the sagebrush, eyes sparkling in the shadows as they run effortlessly for night.

Food is fuel but miles kill appetite. Too often I can't think of what I want to eat when faced with rack after rack of bewilderingly unfamiliar snacks, so resort to Coke and M&Ms. Simple calories that slip down unnoticed, bright enough to be toys. McDonald's and Subway are saviours: often back to back in the malls that line the strips, they allow me to buy and eat the first half of a sub, then move next door for one or two double cheeseburgers and a vanilla shake while stashing the second half of the sandwich in my pack for supper. Starbucks is double Frappuccinos with extra cream and sugar; roadside diners mean pancakes, eggs and hash browns; gas stations are ice-cream sandwiches at nearly 1,000 calories apiece. Yet still I get thinner and thinner until my quads and calves look painted on and my ribs make shadow ladders beneath my skin.

Long miles wreak havoc on a rider's body and the 10,000 miles of preparation only attempt to minimize the effects, not eliminate their cause. Saddle-sores and chafing are inevitable when you're riding over 100 miles a day, blisters and numbness, scratches and scrapes. The tan lines are incredible and are still there a year later but long miles hurt. The pain they inflict is something you can either cope with or you can't. My mind is tougher than my body, and as the race wears on I ride standing every morning for 10 miles, sometimes more, before the painkillers and resolution kick in and sitting on the saddle becomes bearable again.

Climbing Colorado's Meaden Peak takes a long push up an unrideable trail, wet with snowmelt and slush, a boulder-strewn cliff in the pool of my light. The endless shoving of uncooperative wheels and relentless twisting of a tired back drags on tendons, knee pain building horrifyingly rapidly until every step is screaming agony. I bite my lower lip until I taste blood, taking three steps, then two at a time. Then just one, pausing to breathe deeply with every metre crawled and face the doubts head-on. The darkness gets deeper, outside and in, and fear starts to nibble at my heels.

I must go faster, yet I'm too tired. I need to rest, but it's too cold to stop up here at 10,000 feet. I have to keep going, even though every step rips down my leg, taking my confidence with it. It's just a matter of hanging on. The descent is just as painful, though mercifully faster; hanging on to the bars and gritting my teeth, I tell myself I'm covering distance now and this is A Good Thing. Make it to Steamboat and you can stop. Bribery, coercion. Hold on till Steamboat. Nearly there.

At the next junction, still miles from Steamboat but conceivably off the mountain, I unroll the sleeping bag, pull on all my clothes and crawl into sleep beside comforting tyre tracks in the dirt, dragging my wrecked limbs behind me through freezing dreams. Waking before dawn and staring at the stars, I stretch gently beneath the layers and it's as if the night's hell had never happened. Everything is fine again and I roll down the hill toward coffee and breakfast with a grin of relief on my face.

Dawns on the Divide are wonderful times. Feeling the warmth of the first sunray as it slips between the mountains, the spirit lift that comes with the day's opening glow and the peace in its gradually diminishing departure – all of these things are what make the frequent pain and the tedium only incidental and quickly forgotten. There is a magic in experiencing every dawn, dusk and the moments in between that allows you to appreciate the passage of time that's diminished by four walls and a roof over your head.

Occasional overnights in motel rooms mean hot water and a chance to scrub my blackened limbs until they sting with cleanliness but inevitably I wake in the early hours, scared by the humming silence of double-glazed windows and distant traffic. The greatest joy is to leave these places and pedal out under the sky, ready for the day to begin, feeling the breeze start to lift with the sunrise and knowing that you've earned another fresh start to your life.

I realize quickly that returning to normal ways is going to be very hard indeed and I struggle with anything which connects me to what now seems like someone else's life. The mandatory phone-ins are painful. (Riders must phone race HQ every 24 hours or so to confirm that they're still OK and haven't got irreparably lost or eaten by bears. No, really.) Even though I have so much to say to the few I hope are listening, I find myself empty-headed and numb when hooked up to the crackling static, stuttering more than usual and struggling to get the words out. I navigate the frustrations of calling cards once to phone home and speak to my mother, standing outside a gas station staring at the mountains and imagining the English summer rain she says is hammering the windows. She sounds tired and far away and I know that she's worried, that I am putting her through hell as I disappear literally off the map for hours and sometimes days, but I also know she understands what I can't give up, even for love.

After the call ends I sit for an hour on the forecourt in the sun, watching men in jeans and cowboy boots come and go in their trucks. Drained by the effort of sounding sane, shepherding my thoughts into coherence, I wonder whether the absolute selfishness a task like this requires makes me a bad person. My musings lead me in circles and back to the point where I started: I have experienced more happiness in the past few days than I have in years and therefore it can't be wrong.

I am a self-contained unit – everything I need right now is strapped to my two wheels and I can ride in and out of other people's lives, passing through them and taking little, leaving no trace. It's a simple and seductive existence and I think rarely of my life in boxes back in the UK. I do miss my friends and often wish they were here but in the bottom of my backpack is a small dry bag that I don't open once for the duration of the trip. In it are my iPod, my mobile, my passport and a £20 note. There are also notes, drawings and photos from home, carefully folded to 6 inches square. The bag is marked *ICE*, more to make a point for my own benefit than that of potential rescuers, and though it doesn't see the light of day until I'm holed up in Oregon recovering, the knowledge that I carry the love and wishes of my friends with me is sustaining.

As the miles roll on, the Divide crossings mount. At some there are signs and I lean my bike against the post to take a picture. I have a vague plan to frame each and every one to remind myself of where I've been but I miss the Divide so much when I'm done that I can't bear to look at the pictures and they sit on a card gathering digital dust for months and months. When I eventually load the files, I find that they tell only half the story and that my memories are just as vivid as the moment in which they were encountered. Words scrawled in the sand in New Mexico by friends and fellow racers who had passed hours before, hightailing it to the end. Blue spiders raising menacing forelegs under torchlight and the dog-sized hares who kept watch in the Basin. Rolling high with a tailwind over the Divide at 3 a.m., lying on my back in the sagebrush and failing to count even an inch of the stars. The dry scent of forests that see more sunshine than cloud, the smell of hot rain and lightning in the badlands above Del Norte. The crunch of snow underfoot and the hammering of washboard. The sunset howling of wolves in the Gila and the hollow thunder of cattle running unseen through darkness along the long road to Mexico. The bittersweet and beautiful final sunrise.

Somebody wrote, not too long ago, that those who ride the fastest, the hardest and the furthest have something to ride away from. The Divide made me believe that they've found something to ride to. Even if it's just another sunrise.

PEA AND GRAVEL SOUP

JULIE ANNE CHRISTY

Julie Anne Christy climbed her first mountain aged five, wearing a yellow rubber raincoat in outback Western Australia. Years of surfing and beach adventures followed, but it was always the mountains that she was drawn to, despite having less than average and often inappropriate gear.

Her adventures include backcountry skiing in Alaska, hiking in Mexico, surfing in shark-infested waters in Australia and being a certified snake handler. Despite this list of accomplishments, she insists she is not a "badass" and is often the slowest and least skilled person on her trips. She just likes to say yes, and is often scored 10/10 for enthusiasm!

Julz is also a registered nurse and works part-time for the emergency services. She has linked her two passions of mental wellness and the outdoors with Her Mountain Calls, a scholarship programme which gets deserving women who may not normally get the chance for outdoor adventures to experience a dose of nature, supported by female-led outdoor professionals.

For her own sanity, Julz spends some time every day in her local hills with her hairy husband and her even hairier dog, Badger.

You can keep up with Badger's adventures at @furtherfasternz.

"What do you mean, address? I told you already – I am near a road 9 kilometres east of the Mundaring traffic lights on the Great Eastern Highway."

I was lying on my back, struggling to talk to the lady at the end of the emergency services phone line.

"I'm sorry, Julie, but I need your street address to find you."

For some reason I was a little exasperated when I replied, "Look, I'm in the bush, alone, and my handlebars are inside me!"

Those were the last words I uttered into my mobile that day.

There I was, lying on the ground, unable to move, wedged between my bike, a grass tree and a nest belonging to many thousand meat ants. Random thoughts flashed through my mind: *Am I going to bleed to death? I'd really like a flat white. Don't burn the milk, thanks.*

———

That morning had been an early start to beat the heat that penetrates the Perth Hills in February. I headed on to the trail with my Kiwi mate, Mike. Most weekends Mike and I would explore a trail around Perth with our bikes and grab a coffee and breakfast on the way home before the sun got too hot.

Pea and Gravel Soup   Julie Anne Christy

This morning we decided to ride a loop or two of Forsyths Mill, famous for pea gravel and having Western Australia's first shore-style feature.

Arriving with the sun still softly golden, rising up through the gum trees, we rode the first loop together. The track was becoming drier and the loose pea gravel caught us both out at times. Not really knowing who would be taken by the gravel's charms next, we took turns riding ahead of each other, with just a holler or yelp coming when things got a little hairy. As I rounded a tight corner, a tree trunk caught my bars, almost putting me on the ground. I caught up with Mike in a minute or so, only to hear that he had just landed briefly in a tree as well. We chuckled and rode on.

"Fancy another loop of the trail?" Mike asked.

My tummy was growling and my sports drink was just not cutting it – but not to ride the loop again? Well, that would be cheating in my mind!

"Yes," I declared.

The sunrise was pretty special, and I held back to enjoy the serenity and the pleasure of spending time alone in the bush while Mike enjoyed being a speed demon, riding well ahead of me. The sunrise was glorious, but my body was telling me it was coffee o'clock. While having a little dream about my post-ride flat white, I skidded out on the pea gravel again; the trail was flat and more of an access road at this point. Nothing dangerous or wild. How I skidded in such mundane conditions I am not sure – however, the pea gravel has a way of turning regular dirt into a sea of marbles. My back tyre slid beneath me, my bike hit a tree, which bounced my front tyre into a native grass tree, the front of my bike spun around, and somehow I ended up in the dirt underneath my trusty steed.

Lying on the ground, the thought crossed my mind that this was a bigger crash than usual and I tried to get up. Only this time I *couldn't* get up. It turns out this was a MUCH bigger crash than usual.

This was where my nurse's instincts took over. Broken leg? Possibly. I looked down and tried to move my leg off my bike only to see my brake lever was somehow under my shorts. Odd, I know, so I pulled on the lever, but it wouldn't move either. That's when it hit me. The lever was deep, deep inside my thigh, right next to my femoral artery. The lack of blood was confusing, but alas, my trusty bike had great components, and the lever had managed to plug the hole it had made!

My calls for help were to no avail. It seems it is true: when you are alone in the bush, no one can hear you scream. I managed to wiggle my backpack off and call for an ambulance. Luckily for me, another rider, Sarah, came around the bend, God bless her merino socks. She was as shocked as me, and needed firm direction about how my recovery and rescue were going to go, but being dazed and confused from the crash I decided now was a good time for someone else to take over the rescue op. Luckily, she knew the actual address of where we were located, and after I threw my phone at her she was able to tell the ambulance service the correct address (Gorrie Road off the Great Eastern Highway in case you were wondering). The St John Ambulance team were on their way!

Dozing in and out of consciousness, Sarah and I somehow managed the situation so I was not left alone. Sarah contacted Mike and got him on ambulance alert so he could direct them to me, and Sarah was on meat-ant duty. There is nothing like a colony of wild Western Australian ants eating from the grazes and cuts on your arms and groin to distract you from the fact that a good chunk of your handlebar is inside your leg.

The paramedics arrived by bike, leaving the ambulance by the road as it couldn't manage the drive up the trails. By this time I was pretty much out for the count, concussion kicking in. The paramedics started to pull my bike apart, with me still attached. It was clear it was going to be a tough job for them and me, and so they kindly dosed me up with some ketamine to ease the situation. This was the point I saw the bright lights that people talk about on TV, but it was more like a psychedelic highway than the gates of heaven that I'd imagined. I wondered if I had clipped my femoral artery and if this was the end, death being the next chapter. However, suddenly I woke up as I was being loaded from the back of a bike-trail maintenance vehicle and into a helicopter.

My left leg took quite a beating. The lever just missed my femoral artery, but it did knock my femoral nerve quite a bit. The pain was unlike anything I had experienced before. I had surgery at the State Major Trauma Unit, but also spent an hour prior as a sideshow exhibit so all the doctors and nurses could get a good look at "that nurse with the handlebars stuck in her leg". Surgery over, and I was still alive.

The next day I was still in hospital and my leg still wouldn't move. I asked everyone when it would get better. "Soon" was the same response I got from the surgeon, physiotherapist, nurses and registrars, my parents, husband, sister and friends. I was confused as "soon" came and went and still I couldn't move most of my leg. By the third day I realized I could move some of my foot and toes. My quadriceps didn't seem to exist no matter how hard I tried to make them move, and I was still not sure what was actually wrong with me. I could stand on my good leg, but I would fall like a game of Jenga if I balanced on my left leg. My leg was flaccid, like a hock of ham from the deli. After a few days a kind physiotherapist came to see me, and seeing as my foot still worked, she told me she could help get me moving. She put me in a huge hinge brace, set at zero degrees, so I was like a peg leg, with no bending. She gave me a wheelie trolley to balance on, and that was it! I was off and racing, up and down the corridor in my huge brace and with a huge smile! A few days of practising and I graduated to crutches.

Soon I was annoying everyone by hobbling up and down the trauma ward and they told me I could go home that night. They still didn't say what was wrong with me, except that I should get better soon and that I needed some more tests in three weeks once the swelling went down. I was elated! I could go home!

Arriving home was a shock. Everything that was once easy was now hard or impossible. Toilet? Shower? Being able to balance still enough to make toast? All these things landed me in struggle town, and still I didn't know what was wrong with me. After my concussion subsided a little, I started to read the medical journals I had access to from working at the hospital. This was when I realized what was wrong with me: it had loads of different fancy names but what it meant to me in reality was that my left quadricep was paralyzed. When I was at the hospital and the doctors said I should get better "soon", I thought maybe that afternoon or in a few hours. But the more I read, it became apparent that "soon" meant years, and possibly not at all.

———

"Quick!! Quick!! Hurry uuuuupppp!!!" Unable to hold the elation, I was hollering out much louder than I needed to, seeing as my sister and mum were in the next room.

They both came running in, bewildered as to what could be so important.

"Look here! It moved!!" I said, pointing at my left leg, wasted, shrivelled and limp from months of no use.

Again, I moved my leg. I felt a tremor above my knee... Did I? I thought I did – I was sure of it. But then nothing.

No one could see anything... nothing moved. No tremor, no wiggle and the recent conductivity tests from the neurologists all indicated that the nerves were still as paralyzed as they were the day the bike went into me months ago. With my outbursts of "It's moving!", I knew my family were starting to worry about my sanity.

I looked up at Mum, seeking approval and recognition, and she gave me a pitying smile, "Oh, Julie. Maybe soon."

After months of rehab, specialists and stress on my family, maybe it was time I accepted that my left quadriceps were paralyzed, that walking, running and moving freely unassisted were in the past, and now was the time to focus on moving on.

So I kept quiet. I kept doing my exercises and visualization exercises to fire the neural pathways I read about in the medical journals, but I didn't make a song and dance about it. I did them in private.

A few weeks later I felt it again. Then again the next week. The following week there was a distinct twitch in my leg. A definite twitch. I was not crazy – I could see it with my own eyes. I booked myself in to see the neurosurgeon, who fitted me in on a last-minute appointment before he headed off on holiday to watch the Tour de France, as I needed confirmation that I was not imagining it. He gave me the formal acknowledgement I needed to hear: that I was going to heal. Slowly, he said, but he was sure I was going to recover to 80–90 per cent of my original function.

I was ecstatic! I celebrated by heading to my local independent bike shop, Wembley Cycles, and saw the boys. They had a new ruby-red-and-white carbon racing specialized women's mountain bike in the window. Not only was she very pretty with shiny spokes and jet-black tyres – she also had much smaller brake levers! I still needed help with moving about, and so the boys lifted me on to the bike and wheeled me around the parking lot to make sure she fitted and that I could ride her with ease once I was recovered.

With my diagnosis changed from paralysis to severe neuropraxia (a temporary loss of motor and sensory function), I was full of hope despite still being immobile. With a bit of help from my husband, I got my new bike hooked up to the wind trainer. He would help me get on the bike and then strap the foot of my bad leg to the pedals so I didn't fall off. My good leg would push and pull the pedals, and my bad leg would follow, strapped along, going with the flow. I was away pedalling, sweating and loving every moment of it. I was cycling in my dining room listening to my headphones – it was not the trails and birdsong I dreamed of, but it was a start and I was bloody happy!

I wasn't sure where to end this story, but that's because the story never really ended. The next eight months were bewildering if nothing else. I went from being told I may never walk unaided again to finishing my first ever cross-country bike race on my beautiful ruby-red bike. I may have finished last, with my leg flopping about at times, and having to take much longer with only limited power in my quadriceps that were still recovering, but I finished. It was the biggest high of my life.

I stop and smile every time I realize how lucky I have been. It has also been bloody hard work, with constant rehab. "Normal" people asked me why on earth I was back on the bike, but normal people in my world love riding as much as I do and don't need to be told. They know that being on the bike, out on the trails, in the woods and on the hilltops is my home, a part of me. It is just that now, the not-too-hot flat white comes before *and* after every treasured ride, with an added Afghan biscuit and not as many ants since I moved to New Zealand.

TRULY TOUGH
KATE RAWLES

Dr Kate Rawles is passionate about using adventurous journeys to help raise awareness and inspire action on our most urgent environmental challenges. She has recently completed The Life Cycle: an 8,288-mile, largely solo ride the length of South America on a bamboo bike that she built herself. En route she explored biodiversity: what it is, what's happening to it, why it matters and what can be done to protect it.

A former university lecturer, Kate now works freelance as a public speaker, writer and activist. Her book, *The Carbon Cycle: Crossing the Great Divide*, was shortlisted for the Banff Mountain Festival Adventure Travel Book Award in 2013. Other "adventure plus" journeys include the Gyre to Gaia ocean plastic pollution sailing voyage with Pangaea Exploration.

Kate lives in Cumbria with her partner, Chris. She is a fellow of the Royal Geographical Society, a member of The Adventure Syndicate and an Ibex Earth biodiversity ambassador. She holds sea kayaking and mountain leader qualifications.

Find out more about Kate at:
W: www.outdoorphilosophy.co.uk
T: @CarbonCycleKate
I: @carboncyclekate
F: @biodiversitybikeride

In 2017–18 I spent 13 months cycling the length of South America on a bamboo bike I'd built myself. I rode most of it alone and my route largely followed the spine of the Andes, the longest mountain chain in the world. My journey was called The Life Cycle and the overall aim, alongside the opportunity for an extraordinary, life-affirming personal adventure, was to use the story of the journey to help raise awareness and inspire action on one of the biggest and yet least understood and publicized environmental challenges of our time: biodiversity loss.

We are losing species at such a rate it has been called "the sixth great extinction", caused, for the first time in the history of our planet, by a single, resident species – us. Biodiversity, the astonishing variety of species we share the planet with – from starfish to great whales, from the microorganisms in our soil to great oak trees, from kingfishers to fireflies, anteaters to elephants, jaguars to jellyfish – is our life support system, the web of life we are part of and utterly dependent on. And yet most of us barely know what it is.

My goal was to explore all of this alongside the mountains and other amazing landscapes and ecosystems – deserts, rainforests and everything in between – that my journey was to take me through. As well as witnessing some of our planet's rich variety of life and habitats first-hand, I would visit a diverse range of projects and people who I hoped would help me unpack some key questions. What is biodiversity? What's happening to it? Why does this matter? And, above all, what can we do to protect it? I would blog and post about what I found as I travelled. And then, when I got back, I would use the journey as the basis for articles, talks, film clips and eventually a book – all about biodiversity and all (hopefully!) rendered engaging and accessible and action-inspiring by the adventure story they were rooted in.

I think of this journey-with-a-purpose approach as "adventure plus". The ethical outdoor gear company Patagonia calls it "adventure activism". Whatever the name, it wasn't my first crack at it. Among other adventure-plus escapades, I'd cycled from Texas to Alaska following the spine of the Rockies. The environmental focus of that trip, The Carbon Cycle, was climate change, and it was darkly fitting to ride through two of the most oil-intensive, oil-addicted countries on earth – at the height of the Bush administration in the USA's case. President Bush seems scarily benign now, but at the time he was perceived as the arch-villain of the climate change drama. In the course of The Carbon Cycle I talked to all sorts of people, from truck drivers to ranchers to energy-conservation campaigners, about what they thought about climate change, and how they thought we should be responding. I sought out the solutions coming from the belly of the oil beast. And then I took it all home to the UK, using the journey as the basis of numerous slideshows and a book.

The aim was to use the adventure story to reach new audiences; to help open up and move forward our own conversations about climate change and how to tackle it – conversations which were, of course, much less frequent and developed in 2006 than they are now. I love the combination of adventure and environmental purpose and its exciting, energizing potential for the real, positive, much-needed change that happens when people and communities understand the importance of an issue, and their own power to do something about it. More than that, the social transition needed to tackle both climate change and biodiversity loss – to move toward real sustainability – is an adventure we are all on, wittingly or otherwise. We stand a much better chance of success if we rise to the spirit that the notion of "adventure" summons, and embrace the challenge.

But, despite having both passion and a track record, for The Life Cycle I was ill equipped on multiple levels. The Carbon Cycle was by then over ten years in the past. My long-distance cycling skills and memories and wisdom and instincts were all rusty and I was physically in less than peak shape. My Spanish was terrible. Biodiversity is a huge and almost overwhelmingly complex, urgent topic. And then there was the bike. Woody, who I built over a week on a "how to build a bamboo bike" course at the Bamboo Bicycle Club in London, was made from bamboo from the Eden Project in Cornwall, and was an icon of sustainability. But, alongside a lot of banter about his less than conventional – some would say less than beautiful – appearance, there were serious question marks about whether he would actually hold together. My journey would be long – I would be away for over a year – and loaded up with camping kit plus laptop (among other clobber). The bike would be carrying a lot of weight, off and on road in all sorts of weather conditions. And I am a rubbish mountain biker. Would the bike cope?

―――――

It will come as no surprise, then, that to say "I learned a lot" would be a massive understatement. Perhaps more surprising is the what. One of the main things I learned was this: toughness didn't really come into it, or at least not directly. My journey was not tough. I am not tough.

Don't get me wrong. In among the amazing encounters with landscapes, animals, people and projects there were a lot of miles, a lot of hills, a lot of heat, a lot of headwinds, a lot of tiredness and a fair amount of sheer, downright exhaustion. A section of southern Bolivia, for example. After the incomparable high of cycling across the salt flats, a landscape like no other on earth – the flats appear on the horizon like a hard, white ocean, and then you cycle on to it, crunching over the salt hexagons into the huge whiteness – I turned for the Eduardo Avaroa National Park. I'd been given a lift to the edge of the park, dropped off in the bitterly cold, vivid blue early morning. I'd no idea, really, whether I could make the four-day-ish ride across it or whether I was carrying enough water and could cope with the condition of the road. But I passionately wanted to see the *Laguna Colorada* (coloured lake) and the flamingos who live there.

The Laguna Colorada is part of a gigantic good news story: a 1.4-million-hectare reserve, designated as a Ramsar site (i.e. of immense importance to wetland birds) in 2009. Three of the world's six flamingo species can be found in the reserve, including 60 per cent of the entire population of the James's flamingo, a bird which was once thought extinct and is still extremely rare. I had visited many, many biodiversity-related projects by this point – somewhat over halfway through my journey in terms of miles and quite a bit further in terms of time – and while many of the people I'd met were downright inspirational, the stories they told about the systemic degradation of critical habitats, from forests to wetlands to high mountain *páramo*, had left me with a conflicting mix of emotions, including anger, despair, determination, impotence and a powerful urge to act. Right then I very much wanted to be somewhere where conservation was working. And that was, quite simply, straightforwardly beautiful.

Laguna Colorada exceeded my hopes. The lake, streaked orange and magenta, and the flamingos, delicately pink and in their thousands, were among the most beautiful things I'd ever seen. Thousands of other birds swept through the skies around the lake too. It was biodiversity at its most vivid and most spectacular; the high-vis tip of the biodiversity iceberg above the myriad of small or invisible life forms that hold it all together beneath the surface and that make life possible for all species, including us. It was definitely worth the detour involved to be there.

And then it got gnarly. The road was gravel, often thick gravel, and washboardy. I couldn't ride much of it, and when I could it was a literal boneshaker. There were constant mean, sharp climbs. It was all at altitude. And, of course, there was a headwind. Frozen nights in the tent and long, hard days. Out of those four days I must have pushed the bike – and all the gear on it – through deep, corrugated gravel for a good two and a half of them. One day, after working myself almost to exhaustion, my average speed was 1.6 miles per hour. Utterly disheartening. At some point around then, I let the bike fall to the ground and, for the first time on the entire journey, sat down and cried. *I can't go on. I can't go on...* After a while, looking around at the high, dry desert around me, the inevitable inner question arose. *OK then, so what are you going to do?* I picked up the bike and carried on, a bit surprised to find that I felt better for having had a good sob.

———

I popped out of the national park at a place that must be on the list of most remote border posts in the world, a small grey hut hunched on that part of the artificial line between southern Bolivia and Chile. The hut was followed by wonderful smooth tarmac that I did actually kiss (I became embarrassingly enamoured of tarmac, for an environmentalist), the tarmac in turn followed by the most welcome road sign in the world – that sign that shows a truck poised at the top of a fabulously steep descent. Downhill! Downhill straight into a desert tourist town, an extended cafe break and a lot of refuelling.

In terms of hard riding, Bolivia was only capped by Patagonia, a region so windy that the wind has its own roadsigns. I was in a rush at this point, racing time south to make it to Ushuaia in Argentina before I needed to head back north to catch my cargo ship home. I was riding all the hours I could, as hard as I could, and constantly doing the maths – at this speed, with this number of hours per day, I'll get to Ushuaia... aagh. The maths simply wasn't adding up. Just when the side wind became so ferocious I was struggling to keep the bike on the road, it would turn into a headwind and I'd pretty much come to a halt if not go backward. I learned to dread the bends in the road that would funnel me inexorably from an impossible side wind into a beyond impossible headwind.

Yet I somehow couldn't give up. Despite the apparent impossibility of reaching it on time, I could not find a way of redesignating the end point that didn't feel like failure, and I couldn't bring myself to just quit either. I had made an almost entirely arbitrary decision, months ago, in comfort somewhere, that the end of my journey would be Ushuaia. Worse, I had announced this on Facebook. That decision had now trapped me in my very own, entirely clichéd, race-to-the-finish narrative.

Then, right at the last minute, the wind changed direction. I rode a tailwind for 99 miles without stopping, and finally cracked the maths, arriving into Ushuaia with one day left in which to make all the travel arrangements to get me and Woody back to Santiago in time to catch the ship home. (Two ferries, three long-distance buses and one very expensive taxi – don't ask. But I had crossed the Atlantic by ship in order to reduce my own carbon emissions, which it did very significantly in comparison to flying, and I wasn't about to hop on a plane now.) For weeks I'd been working so hard physically that my leg hair, toe and fingernails had all stopped growing and the hair on my head, thick and wild at the outset, was all thin and straggly. But I'd made it. Made it to Ushuaia, the town they call "the end of the world". I've never been so exhausted nor so exhilarated to arrive anywhere in my life.

———

None of this was tough. Not truly tough. Not the days of falling straight off the bike with tiredness and into my tent; not the evenings of uncertainty about finding a hostel or a safe and hidden place to camp; not the washboard gravel roads nor the relentless, soul-destroying headwinds nor the almost constant hunger. Nor trying to juggle all of this with setting up project visits and emails and staying on top of blogs and journals. I was reminded constantly of my non-toughness in myriad ways, but I learned it most vividly through two encounters.

The first was with a young woman running a roadside food stall in northern Colombia. The stall was one of a handful on that stretch of road, colourful but scantily stocked – mostly biscuits and cartons of sweetened fruit juice. I stopped because she smiled; bought a packet of coconut biscuits and ate them there and then, wondering how on earth a family could make a living from such a stall – her mother sat in shadows in a back room – and chatting as best I could in my bad Spanish.

The young stallholder was called Lola and she really wanted to see my passport. It seemed an odd request and responding was going to be mildly embarrassing. I've lost two passports in my life so far and was on my final warning. (A very stern letter accompanied the most recent replacement. It read: "Please be advised that this passport is the property of Her Majesty's Government. If you lose another one, it will not be replaced.") I was cycling with my passport in a plastic bag inside an unpleasantly stained and constantly-damp-if-not-wet super-safe passport-holding waist belt under my clothes against my skin. The plastic bag protected it from the sweat, though not entirely. I dug it out. Lola took the small, clammy, maroon object and turned it over and over in her hands. When I left, passport back in its belt, she gave me a beautiful bunch of dark purple grapes, a truly generous gift from someone who had so little.

It only occurred to me later that she might never have seen a passport before. She almost certainly didn't have one. What must it have represented to her, in terms of freedom? The wealth gap between us was as much to do with options as it was with money. I could travel through her country, but she was utterly unlikely ever to travel through mine. She would probably never leave Colombia. Quite possibly she would never leave that stall.

The second encounter was among the most powerful in my life, and a whole lot darker. Jennifer, another young Colombian and a single mum, was part of a small group of people, all in their twenties, from Cajamarca: a high mountain town in one of the most fertile farming regions of Colombia. Jennifer was the ultimate David in the ultimate David and Goliath story. Goliath was AngloGold Ashanti, one of the biggest gold-mining corporations in the world, based in South Africa, with a terrible human rights record and operating in Colombia with its own private army. AngloGold were proposing to open a gold mine in the area so large it was called *la Colosa* (the Colossal One). Mercury is used in the extraction of gold from rocks – about a tonne of rock has to be unearthed for less than a gram of gold – and this and other heavy metals leach inexorably into the soil and water, causing fantastically dangerous amounts of contamination, making the area unfarmable and the water undrinkable. The contamination continues for thousands of years after the gold-mining operations have finished – gold-mining in this way is an ecocide. *La Colosa* would decimate the farming community and the ecosystems and water sources all around it.

Jennifer and her group decided that they couldn't just sit back and watch this happen. They decided to resist. They organized a meticulously researched information campaign to counter the disinformation and denials coming from AngloGold. Then, after years of this work, travelling to all the local villages and farms, they arranged for a public referendum to take place on whether the community wanted the gold mine or not.

Somewhere during this process, two of the group, two young lads, were assassinated. One was shot at a party. The other found hung. The rest carried on. And they won the referendum by an overwhelming majority despite various (relatively minor) skulduggeries by the pro-mining mayor, including handing out pens with disappearing ink for the ballot.

The outcome of public referendums are legally binding in Colombia but, when I met Jennifer, neither she nor her group knew whether AngloGold or the Colombian government would respect the result. "We'll carry on anyway," she said. "And if, after we've exhausted every democratic avenue open to us, AngloGold are still here, then we will fight." A handful of young people against a multinational company with its own army, operating with the blessing of the Colombian government? That would not end well.

Some time after meeting Jennifer, I heard the brilliant news that AngloGold had packed up and gone. The region is now strengthening its farming and tourism industries, and Jennifer's group advises other communities fighting similar battles against environmentally devastating forms of mining. Huge financial wealth (for some) is generated via this kind of mining, but the costs can be far, far too high. Costs to people and to the environment – to ecosystems, to biodiversity, to soil and to water, none of which we can live without. Water for gold – or for lead, or copper, or oil – is a very bad exchange.

I was deeply affected by meeting Jennifer. Since I've been back, though, I've learned that her story, tragically, is not unique. While Colombia, and indeed the whole of South America, is a fabulous place to travel as a tourist or a random cyclist (I had not one whiff of trouble the whole time I was there, and I met no other cyclists who had had any either), it is a desperately dangerous place to be an environmentalist or a human rights activist. The third most dangerous in the world, in fact, according to Global Witness, who, in conjunction with *The Guardian* newspaper, have been holding witness to the work, lives and deaths of "environmental defenders" around the world. In 2007 alone, 197 were killed. That's nearly four a week.

And so, without in any way seeking to downplay the importance of still much-needed gender-stereotype-busting and all the other achievements of all of us so-called "Western" women out there who push ourselves; who travel in marginal ways and who climb or bike or ski or swim or run hard; who sleep in tents and bivvies, and who cope with heat and coldness and exhaustion and uncertainty and self-doubt and crazy challenges of multiple forms... we are there, in the main anyway, by choice. We typically have passports – an astonishing privilege in itself – and options. Lots of options. And, while many of us may operate on very small budgets, relatively speaking, almost all of us have an emergency credit card in a back pocket somewhere and could likely get out if we needed to. We put ourselves in these toughness-generating, toughness-requiring situations. It's a choice. At the very least, it's a privileged toughness, if it's toughness at all.

I grew up as a weedy scrap of a kid. I was in many ways a bit of a wimp, and still am if I'm really honest, though I've always aspired to be tough for reasons I can't quite figure out and probably wouldn't much like if I did. Since meeting Jennifer and Lola, though, I've had a vivid inner wince when anyone calls me tough, or says my journey was tough – when I'm paid the compliment I've been hankering after for decades.

No. True toughness is when you are struggling to eke out a living from a failing roadside stall and don't know what else to do, and yet you offer generosity to passing strangers, interacting with curiosity and warmth. True toughness is shown by the people whose life choices are massively constrained, through no fault of their own.

True toughness is enduring the impact of the sixth great extinction and the climate change emergency – no rain, too much rain, failing crops, failing water supplies, violent weather, floods, droughts, spread of diseases, infertile soil, dying forests, dying animals, dying fish, loss of your land, ecosystem collapse – when you've done very little or nothing to cause them. We've all got these terrible challenges ahead of us, though our Western lifestyles have done a lot more to contribute to them than those of the Jennifers and Lolas of the world, and will insulate us from them for longer.

True toughness is not just enduring these catastrophes you haven't caused but doing your utmost to work out how to turn this all around. It is putting your all into trying to figure out how best to fight for the positive even if your options seem few; how to protect the people and land and wildlife and community that you love and need, knowing that you may be putting your life on the line, literally, but carrying on anyway.

True toughness is being an environmental defender. It is taking on an earth-decimating, militarily armed multinational when you are a single mum with next to nothing. It is having at the front of your mind, vividly, all the time, what many of us have long forgotten: nature is our life support system. We need it. It is not a luxury. We cannot live without it. Nature is a community of other beings who deserve to be here every bit as much as we do – a community we belong to and utterly depend on.

True toughness is living with the knowledge of what's happening to it and fighting for positive change on behalf of all of us, no matter what the personal cost. Whether or not there really is a choice.

————

Two Postscripts

First. On the topic of privileged toughness. Coming back. Wow. After over a year on the road, moving most days, sleeping somewhere different most nights, outside most of the day and often in the tent at night... After that, to be back in a stationary house, with walls, the same house, night after night... After all that motion, to be suddenly stationary felt like a collision. Like hitting a wall. And in among the obviously wonderful reconnections with family and friends and landscapes and animals, the slow, inexorable, heartbreaking loss of gratitude. On the road, every mouthful of food, every glug of water is just fabulous. A good coffee is a miracle. Or a hot shower. Or clean clothes. Or an extended, sparky, interesting conversation in your own language.

I fought against taking these things for granted once I could have them whenever I liked. I tried to *practise* gratitude. But when you can have all these things and more multiple times a day it is hard, really hard, to retain that huge, life-enhancing sense of appreciation. Appreciation for the basic, good stuff of life and not wanting more than that – this is the secret to both happiness and sustainability. So simple and yet so tough to sustain off the bike, off the road, living in a more or less "normal" way in a "normal" Western culture, with rooms and wardrobes instead of panniers, where stuff and money are taken to trump smiles and conversations, and riding your bike in the hills and chatting with strangers and living with just enough.

There's an easy sense of purpose and meaning on the road too, however illusory: each day is shaped by the need to find food and shelter and to get to wherever you are going. Life is both straightforward and vivid. There's a feeling of being really, truly alive. And also, something harder to articulate: a strange sense, at least sometimes, of somehow tuning in with the overall ebb and flow of things. An intuition of other layers of reality. A feeling, sometimes, that you are in some other-world groove and that, so long as you stop trying to control and just go with it, everything will be just fine. And there is connection – connection with the ordinary extraordinariness of the world. The smile of a stallholder. A kid playing with a dog. Two ducks on a temporary pond in a flooded field. Cycling into a sudden small cloud of floating seed heads. A car with rocking base-beat music roaring past, its passengers laughing and punching the air. The cries of pink flamingos. A gift of grapes. I constantly reach back for those images, and for the feeling of sheer aliveness, and it breaks my heart to watch them recede and fade.

Second. The final distance of The Life Cycle journey was 8,288 miles. Woody the bamboo bike made the whole thing with barely a mechanical fault and is without doubt the most reliable bike I've ever owned. I'll concede this much: that bike is tough.

BUILDING BRIDGES
MISBA KHAN

Misba Khan is a British adventurer who was part of the 2018 all-female Euro-Arabian expedition team to reach the North Pole. An "ordinary mum" turned Rambler turned polar skier, Misba hopes to show people that those of all abilities and from all backgrounds can get involved in activities that may push themselves for their own self-development.

For the past 15 years she has been working as part of the finance team at the North Manchester General Hospital. Aside from her professional role, she is also a trained chaplain, undertaking voluntary work with female patients in the mental health department. Although British born and bred she is of Pakistani origin. She sometimes finds that women in her community are reluctant to stretch their abilities and reach their full potential, and hopes that by sharing her achievements she can encourage others and break down barriers and stereotypes.

Find out more about Misba at:
T: @MisbaNorthPole

It's the first time I've celebrated Pakistan Independence Day actually in Pakistan, my ancestral country. It happens to be a rest day and we're staying in the charming mountain village of Hushe, in the Ghangche District of northern Pakistan. Our small, multinational group has been trekking through the Karakoram mountain range for two weeks now, from where we began in Skardu. We then ascended the Baltoro Glacier and spent a night at K2 base camp. We're near the end of our journey now and some members of the group have chosen to go for a day hike. I'm revelling in the spirit of a rest day, exploring the village and absorbing the adventure of the past fortnight.

I find a quiet spot in the sun to sit and read my book in isolation. I've read *The Magic Faraway Tree* so many times now, but it's different every time I go on an adventure of my own. I'm lost in the pages when the owner of the guesthouse we're staying in approaches and invites me to follow him to the local school, where the Independence Day celebrations are about to commence. His children attend the school and are eager for me to come along.

We walk through the village, stopping to say hello and run errands as we do so. I feel like his daughter, following him somewhat cluelessly, yet curiously, as we visit what feels like every home in the village, greeting neighbours, while he tells me about this place in the gaps in between.

We enter the school to a remarkable reception of children singing in unison. The children are all neatly turned out in their uniforms, which are blue with the girls in white headscarves. The neatness of the children juxtaposes the school's conditions, which are impossible to ignore. It's an incredibly poor building, with no sanitation and limited resources for the children to learn. In a village where almost every adult is illiterate, this is perhaps no surprise, but I still inhale sharply at the sight of the eager youths contrasting against the limited promise offered to them.

Unable to leave Hushe without understanding more about life here, I return to the school after the celebrations to meet with the principal. I sit, once again feeling like a girl, in a low chair across the desk from the man who has charged himself with the task of raising educated children in a village where so few adults have been educated, or even respect education. I wonder if his suit has been donated, the way the sleeves fall down to his knuckles and he fails to fill out the shoulders, yet he is a determined man, passionate about the battle he has taken on. The principal states flatly that within five years of beginning school with him, at least half of the students will have already left and be in fields, working full time.

"It's the older generation who are the problem here," he sighs. "They don't believe in education, because they don't have any and so can't accept any need for it. They're the ones who hold the children back."

After school, I notice him, in his oversized suit, making calls around the village, chatting to citizens about the importance of education, attempting to stoke an ember that could change the future of the local children. Watching him work – tirelessly and against winning odds – fills me with admiration.

I've spent the past decade trying to inspire others around me to get outside and be active, so I understand his hard work. He is trying to change behaviours and go against the grain in order to make the world a better place. I leave Hushe feeling utterly empowered and inspired to work harder when I return home. If this man can believe in a literate population in Hushe, I can grow the numbers of my walking group in northern England.

———

I grew up with Pakistani parents in England, enjoying all of the potential offered to a girl in a Western country, and yet what I'm doing now – an intense, high-altitude trek through the Karakoram range, some of the most formidable mountains in the world – was always beyond my scope and imagination. It wasn't until my own teenage children began their Duke of Edinburgh Awards that this world appeared to me. I saw my children return from trips, dirty and smelling of campfire, filled with a new confidence, each time stronger than when they went out. I wanted some of that for myself. One weekend, I borrowed my daughter's backpack and my son's head torch and went out in Skipton with a walking group. It was a dark, rainy November day and I was outside in the miserable weather with a group of strangers. It was exhilarating.

Two weeks later, I went out with them again, and over the course of the following years began purchasing my own equipment and never missing a group walk if I could avoid it. I built up my confidence, learned how to read a map and realized there was so, so much more of this world that I wanted to see.

And I could see it, if I kept going.

Building Bridges   Misba Khan

In 2017 I joined the first all-female expedition to the North Pole, a record-breaking achievement that had never even been on my radar just a few years prior. It seems almost inconceivable – no, almost irresponsible – to journey in such a short space of time from a simple walk following a group near Skipton to have my name on the records list for reaching the magnetic North Pole. But, like a long hill walk, it is made in single steps. I never missed an opportunity to go out with my walking group. I taught my family to expect nothing from me on Sunday – that was my time to go walking and I would be back later. They just had to do without me for a few hours. They learned to cope, and I expanded my abilities and my love for the outdoors. I gained confidence in navigation, slowly purchased my own equipment (giving my teenagers back their belongings) and showed myself that I could handle bigger challenges. Adventure came late in life for me, but I've grabbed it with both hands.

It was empowering to join that group of strong women on the North Pole expedition, and prove to the world – and ourselves – that women are tough and capable. In the months leading up to our departure, I trained and studied and filled all of my extra hours outside of work and rearing a family with preparing myself to join these women in one of the most hostile and unforgiving places on earth. At some point along this journey, the statement "you'll get this out of your system" was mentioned to me. I felt confused. The truth is, this is now very much in my system. I returned home from our expedition with a hunger for more and the idea of my ancestral country loomed in my mind.

I'm heartbroken saying goodbye to my hosts in Hushe, promising that I'll return as soon as I can – a promise I fully intend to keep. Through my ability to speak Urdu, a second language for the locals, I have been able to connect with so many people during my time in the village, and I leave with a list of phone numbers and Facebook profiles so that I can stay in touch when I return home. While the villagers had seen foreigners here before – so close to the infamous K2 – almost everyone I spoke to had never seen a British Muslim woman before, let alone a foreign trekker who could speak their language. I felt like I was building bridges between West and East. Through the common ground of a religion, I was able to connect on a meaningful level and share so much between two cultures. Maybe it's not the strongest bridge to start building, maybe it's just a small wooden bridge that only a single person can cross, but that's where we start.

We climb out of the village, glittering white peaks flanking either side of us, rising perilously toward the clear blue sky. For nearly two weeks now, we have been on the awe-inspiring Baltoro Glacier. I can hardly grasp the scale of the form we are traversing and every day I pester the resident geologist in our group with new questions, trying to build my understanding. At night in our tents, the noise of the glacier is louder than ever, the constant cracking of ice coming from deep within sounds like the earth itself is opening up. Adding to the noise, we even hear the incredible thunder of avalanches fall in the distance – which suddenly feels very close, lying on my mat with nothing but a sheet of nylon shielding me from the power of the mountains. The rumble and ultimate crash of the avalanches are so loud that it's hard not to imagine they are bound to hit us, although they are actually on mountainsides across the chasm of the valley. I am inspired by the power of nature – inspired by how little I know and empowered by how much I am still able to learn. Two months ago, I had been scared to come on this trip, worried that I wouldn't be able to keep up with the experienced group. Of course I can do this. Of course this is exactly where I'm meant to be.

I bond with our local guides and porters by speaking in Urdu, translating for the rest of the group what they tell me. While I'm eager to learn everything I can about their lives, the landscape here and life in Pakistan, they are equally eager to learn about my life back in the UK. We build more bridges between our two worlds, connecting us across the chasm. At first, they treated me like any other Westerner, but when I approached them to ask for a prayer mat (my luggage restrictions prevented me from bringing my own), they were astonished and delighted to be guiding a Muslim.

It seems hard to believe, at first, that not many Muslim women have trekked through this region, considering that Pakistan is an Islamic country. But the more I uncover about the country, the more I realize how much culture prevents women from exploring and adventuring outside of the bounds of their realm. Women have the hardest jobs in the world. Making and rearing a family is a never-ending task. It's always demanding, there are no statutory holidays and we will always work overtime. We can easily lose our individual selves in this role. It sometimes seems impossible not to.

After 23 days – although I completely lose any grasp on the concept of time – I return to Islamabad and back to the house of my auntie, a professor of geography at Islamabad University. I am stunned when, as I show her photos of my adventure and fill her in on all of the stories, she places her arms on my shoulders and sighs, "Wow, you've been to all of the wonderful places I've only ever heard of and never been."

It's as simple as uploading a few photos to Facebook and telling my friends and family about my trip, but a year later a few of them are planning their own trips around our ancestral country. A small bridge indeed, but it's where we start.

MOSS /
TOUGH SKIN
PAULA FLACH

Paula Flach is a curator, illustrator, writer, and runner with a soft spot for hard weather, combining her passion for the great outdoors with her curiosity for story and connection. After her studies in visual culture and film in Bergen, Norway and Rennes, France, she returned to her native Munich, Germany, where she works as a curator and creative for adventure and outdoor documentaries. She continues to spend her summers up north and generally prefers to wake up in a tent. As an illustrator and writer, she maps experiences and textures of life, turning them into spaces and places on paper. Her illustrations and writing are part of the award-winning *Waymaking* – an anthology of women's adventure writing, poetry and art. Her artwork has been shown in several exhibitions in Germany.

Find out more about Paula at:
W: paulaflach.com
@paula.flach

1: Moss

My hands felt like they had about 2 per cent battery left. They held on to a steel rope and silently damned their owner and gravity. My feet were trying to find some holds on the vertical rock face where I was dangling, trying to push up and also outward to stop my backpack from squishing me against the rock. For some reason I glanced at the insides of my forearms and saw a bit of moss and several small stones sticking to my skin. "Forearms are no place for moss," I thought to myself. Maybe it's the kind of thought that you have when you're in shock. If you have moss on the insides of your forearms, something has gone wrong.

I had flown out to Ålesund, Norway, to visit some friends at their summer hut and spend a few days hiking solo in the iconic and beautiful mountain range of Molladalen. Those were the days of ill-informed packing, predating my love for downsizing my backpack to the bare necessities. The result was that I had packed everything I could possibly need; every apparel from summer shirts to woollen hats and a heavy-duty hard-shell jacket. August in Norway can mean hail and snow, and my pack was around 17 kilograms. While that sounds absolutely mad today, it didn't alarm me at the time. I even took a weird sense of pride in having a big backpack on my shoulders. My friends drove me to the trailhead in the valley, gave me some extra snacks and sent me on my way. Finally alone, I began hiking. After the first few hundred metres I decided to get out my trekking poles, only to realize that one of them had been bent and rendered useless. With nothing to help with the weight of my pack, I scrambled up the valley, with its beautiful beech woods and waterfalls, feeling every single excess kilo on my back.

As the terrain got steeper, the first climby bits appeared ahead. I paused and adjusted my straps. I approached a little via ferrata section that traversed a decent, almost vertical, slab of rock. It looked fine at first, but rain earlier in the day had turned this bit into a temporary waterfall. I edged my way along the rock, holding on to the steel rope that slacked between the bolts. I paid close attention to where I put my feet while being drizzled with icy water from above. I only managed to place the tip of my boots on tiny footholds, while the lax steel rope made me sway with every move.

I must have shifted my weight too quickly on one of the footholds, and my right foot slipped loose. I pulled on the rope as hard as I could. My whole body was fighting the sense of falling. I flexed every muscle to regain balance, my heavy pack only working to pull me down.

Too late.

In an instant, I was dangling in the air. The steel rope tore at the insides of my hands, cold and slippery.

In moments like these I tend to make unflattering growling sounds resembling an aggravated moose or maybe a horny grizzly. The whole of Molladalen must have jumped at the sound of me fighting to find somewhere to place my feet. My boots slipped from the wet rock, my hands started cramping. This was the exact moment when my brain wondered about the moss on the insides of my forearms.

After what felt like a time impossible to measure as time, I regained my footing. I managed to traverse the rock face with throbbing palms and shaky knees.

Once on solid ground again, I sat down against a grassy slope, panting and exhausted, making more growling noises. My palms had shed a good amount of skin and I felt a sting in my abdomen from flexing against the hip belt.

Avoiding the pain, I rummaged in my bag, locating my water and snacks. I did what I had learned to do on other solo adventures: pledge to not think too much about what had just happened.

I call this practice "mental hygiene". After a sticky situation, you brush your mental teeth, use some mental floss if you need to and get back to what you were doing in the first place. It feels rigid, but also helpful and reassuring.

That night I pitched my tent in one of the most beautiful places I've ever camped. It was windy and cold. Still summer in most other parts of the northern hemisphere, in Norway, August is essentially the first month of fall. The wind sent spots of sunlight across the imposing walls of the Molladalstindene mountains (1,414 metres). There were sheets of ice on the lake below. I hadn't seen a human since leaving my friends. This is my happy place: picking a spot for my tent in the solitude of a wild space of lakes and mountains. It was the eve of my 31st birthday and it would be three days before I met another human. I quietly celebrated my birthday by a lake named Brillevatn and stayed in the birthday tent for the majority of a particularly rainy day reading Milan Kundera and eating oatmeal cookies. That trip turned out to be one of the best solo hikes I've done so far. And that sting in my abdomen turned out to be a hernia. Molladalen has made its mark on me. Everlasting memories and three everlasting scars on my belly.

I've been going on solo adventures for the entirety of my adult life. I started out with a solo trip to Norway at 18 – which would later turn it into my home base of choice – and continued with a multi-month trip to New Zealand. The reason I went on these trips by myself was not a conscious choice. My friends from school simply didn't share my enthusiasm for colder climates and most of them went straight to university after graduation. I chose to travel instead. So, I went by myself. In the years since, while I have gone on many trips with friends and significant others, it feels like solo travel is my default method. It's not a question of *if* I go solo, but *where* to go solo.

I was 19 when I quit my job to go to New Zealand for five months. When my employer learned about my travel plans, she took it upon herself to call my parents and alarm them about their daughter's intent to travel halfway across the world, by herself. Luckily, I had been raised in a home where such a reaction was met with a benevolent frown.

Now, in my mid-30s, I see things a bit differently. I notice that I'm more concerned with safety; as if my antennas have become receptive to a different frequency. I even find myself taking a parent's perspective on my adolescent travels and I wonder if I had been in their shoes, would I have behaved the same way my parents did? Back then, I was gone for five months. Until then I had never been away from home for longer than three weeks and I hastened to establish an "I-call-you/you-don't-call-me/no-news-is-good-news" policy before leaving.

My parents never gave me "the talk". And it might sound drastic, but recently I thought, "Huh, they never talked to me about the potential scenario of being robbed or worse."

I recently asked my dad if he and my mum had been more concerned about my safety than about my brothers' and what their rationale for a fairly hands-off approach was at the time. My dad went quiet for a while and then said: "I think it is very simple. We trusted your judgement and that you would use it." And then he added: "And of course, we had to let you go and just hope you'd be fine."

And in an instant it struck me how heartbreaking parenting must be. It struck me that, when you have a kid, you agree to worry about someone for the rest of your life. And if you want to be a good parent, you better not tell them every time you worry about them.

We often frame our stories in the outdoors around our own abilities, our own trials and tribulations. This is not a story about my toughness, but my parents'. The incredible toughness that it requires to trust the world with your child and your child in that world.

And what is more, my father would have said the same thing to my brothers. There was no gender gap in my parents' approach to trusting their sons and their daughter.

My parents had split up a few years before my trip to New Zealand. And I remember that three months into the trip, my dad did breach my "I-call-you/you-don't-call-me/no-news-is-good-news" policy. When he knew where I was staying, he called the hostel and as we spoke, both our voices trembled with suppressed emotion. He had called to hear how I was doing and also to tell me the sweetest of news: that he had fallen in love again. I was happy that he did break my policy.

My parents never gave me the talk. But what they did do was send me and my brothers martial arts training for seven years. And just to be clear, I'm convinced that it would've helped me, if worse came to worst. But maybe it did something about the way I carried myself. In martial arts, just like in any type of sport, you learn what your body can do and how your mind can help. And you learn what your mind can do and how your body can help. And that, to me, is the greatest gift of outdoor adventures and solo ones in particular. Moss on your forearms and hernias included.

2: Tough Skin

I used to have this patch of thicker skin on my right middle finger, where the pencil sits when I'm writing. This tough skin has almost vanished. In the day and age of keyboards and smartphones, typing trumps longhand and while my skin is subtly changed by my dextrous habits, it promptly reacts when habits change too quickly. Which brings me to the most benign (and equally most obnoxious) thing in outdoorsy ventures – blisters.

Blisters on feet, blisters on hands, blisters from running, blisters from rowing, blisters from hiking in shoes too tight, in shoes too loose or just blisters full stop.

A little unhappy patch of skin on your heel can rain on your parade all day every day. A blister can become THE BLISTER on a trip. It's not a matter of blood loss, risk of infection or chance of survival, but the amount of continuous pain inflicted on the careless wanderer can be astounding. I have spent a disproportionate amount of time thinking about blisters, simply because hiking for 7 hours a day lends itself perfectly to obsessive thinking. Or maybe it's not even obsessive thinking. It's just that you're reminded of THE BLISTER every 3 seconds – so every other step. Let the dermatological and mental erosion begin.

Jotunheimen National Park in Norway

It's day two of a seven-day hiking trip in this wild and sublime mountainscape. The word "jotun" stems from Norse mythology and translates as "giant", so Jotunheimen literally means "home of giants". Once you're there, you need not wonder why. Its peaks are the highest in northern Europe and the national park covers more than 3,500 square kilometres. Consider the vastness. A giant's playground comes to mind.

The morning's sunlight has disappeared behind dull midday clouds. The last day of July feels like the last day of April. I trot along the path, marked with red Ts by the trusty members of the Norwegian Trekking Association. I take in the beautiful lines of Rauddal, a valley smoothed over by a gargantuan glacier, but I can hardly hear myself think. As it turns out, glaciers form exquisite wind channels. The howling is barely muffled by my woollen hat. A belligerent headwind chills my bones and keeps pushing me any way but forward.

Wind at this strength always strikes me as frantic.

It makes all things look nervous, the grass, the straps on my pack, the clouds.

It makes me hurry for no reason.

Screaming air.

The incessant flapping of my hood.

The valley ahead – a desert of noise.

Enter the blister.

As I stagger along, I start to feel it on my right heel. And slowly it begins to bicker, throbbing a bit more with every step until I can't ignore it any more. It turns into a commentary on my every move. I can't hear my steps on the ground but I can hear my blister's proclamations of the fact, that it is here by my mistake, that this is horrible already. That 7-hour hikes are not my place. That Rauddal is not my place. And that these boots certainly don't feel like my place. Are we there yet?

Stop.

Sit.

Patch.

Have a snack.

Walk.

Consider THE BLISTER every second step.

Consider the beauty around you in every other step.

Thoughts trail off to greener pastures.

Without me noticing the wind drops.

At the halfway point of the day's distance, I look out across the valley. I marvel at the walls of rock, rising in soft lines from the valley bed. I picture the glacier, lying above all this rock, thick and heavy like a giant's tongue. Thousands of years passed, as the ice willed the rock into beautiful formations with relentless patience. I think of the music of Sigur Rós. If I had to guess, places like these make music like that.

Time and ice. That's all it takes.

Friction, a violent thing. Unforgiving physics.

Water beats rock, with time.

Boot beats skin, with time.

More tape.

Trot on.

How a little patch of skin can turn us into a thin-skinned being altogether.

The sky begins to turn a deeper shade of blue as I reach the hut. The wind has died down completely. The cool air that has torn at me all day is a quiet thing now. It hugs the primeval landscape like a luminescent cape.

I sit down on the porch to take off my boots. I slowly strip my socks off, like peeling a tangerine. Two pale veiny feet emerge, marbled with the imprints of my socks. I can almost hear my toes exhaling. My feet look pinkish in some places, but mostly grey, soaked in sock muck.

What a lot in life, I think, contemplating a foot's existence: stuck in a narrow, dark and damp place most days, pounding pavement and bike pedals, rarely seeing the light of day, unless it's sandal season. Rarely bare, unless it's night-time.

I take a look at my right heel: pink angry skin around the blister patch.

Glue on skin.

The natural and the artificial in an awkward slightly yucky embrace.

All is quiet, in and around me, except for this throbbing aggravated patch of skin.

The day before my right heel was just my right heel. I didn't give it much thought. It was me, part of me, part of the body that is me. Now it is a concern, a nuisance. I think of the next few days and all the steps I know to be ahead. Isn't it curious how quickly we turn a part of ourselves that doesn't work like we're used to into a problem – an object removed from the rest of us?

And with that in mind, isn't it poignant, that the one thing that will heal it, is to stop objectifying it and consider it part of us again?

When my brain is in its out-in-the-elements mode, because my body is out in the elements, I forget most of what is not there. I forget all the books I have read, all the cogs of my daily routine. I forget all the things I own except for what I carry. I sometimes even forget that I'm someone the people in my life know. I forget what my body is used to doing.

My ears don't listen to anything artificial.

My eyes don't read.

My hands don't write.

But that night I sat down to write.

I wrote a poem for my heel.

If you think it's mad to write a poem for your body, I accept the compliment of madness and encourage you to try it.

The poem is in Norwegian and I fail to translate it, but it's essence is the following: My heel and the skin on my heel behold the blister that has come between them – a bubble, which they aren't sure what to do with, but they agree to comfort it and hold it between them till it fades.

The following days I kept returning to the poem in my head and for some reason it helped. It made my blister less of a problem. It was still uncomfortable but with the poem in mind, I stopped regarding the blister as an object, it was just air between my heel and the skin on my heel. The pain changed from being a nuisance, something to get rid of, to something that was also me.

It wasn't just the relief in perception that was satisfying, but also the fact that my body had made my brain write a poem for it. It took some time and friction. Friction on my heel turned into friction in my brain. Pain is erosive, but so is time. And with time, my brain stopped seeing a problem and assumed wholeness instead.

So, for once, my brain had done something for my body, not the other way around. Because, let's be honest, usually my body is reduced to a vehicle for my brain. Because that is how I treat it, when I park it in front of a computer for 8 hours a day. It's supposed to keep still and not complain for those hours until I pick it up and take it home.

My eyes read to feed my brain.

My ears listen for the same reason.

My fingers type to weave networks and uphold connections.

They swipe and tip, zoom and click, buy me seats on trains and aeroplanes, new toys and new connections. They like, they vote, they press for more. My fingers touch a surface made by man to touch the world – but not. They type on keyboards, smartphones, sculpt avatars of me.

And while they forge connections, they are also the epitome of disconnection. We have reduced our physical contact with the world to a minimum – fingertips on a screen.

But the best thing my fingers can do is to touch the world, feel the friction and write a poem in longhand.

MY WHY
REA KOLBL

Rea Kolbl is a professional athlete in love with the outdoors. While her primary sport is obstacle course racing (OCR), she loves any kind of self-propelled motion outside, especially in the mountains. Rea grew up in Slovenia, where sports always played a big part in her life; she was on the national gymnastics team for most of her childhood. After moving to America, she slowly fell in love with trail running, until miles on trails brought her back to her life as an athlete. After finishing her master's in materials science and engineering at Stanford, she moved to Boulder, Colorado, to take a chance on a life as a full-time athlete.

In the past couple of years, Rea has won three 24-hour OCR Ultra World Championships and remains undefeated at endurance OCR of 30 miles or longer. Colorado helped her find a new love of adventure: she also learned how to mountain bike, backcountry ski and climb. Most recently, Rea participated in an expedition adventure race hosted by Bear Grylls in Fiji, a 700-kilometre-plus journey that taught her so much about herself, life and what a true adventure can be like.

Find out more about Rea at:
W: kolblrea.wordpress.com
I: @reakolbl
F: @rkolbl

It was around 8 a.m., and I had been running the same 5-mile obstacle-laden loop for 20 hours. I was climbing up the hill to the top of the cliff dive, barely managing to put one foot in front of the other. I had lost all of my energy gels as I rolled through the mud almost two hours before, and now I wasn't sure I'd make it to the pit stop to restock my supplies and refuel. I knew I didn't have enough energy to walk or jog the extra half-mile penalty to skip the cliff dive – I wasn't sure I'd swim back out if I did take the 40-foot plunge into the lake either. I decided to resolve this dilemma once I climbed to the top – for now, it took all the focus I had to keep moving forward, dizzy from the lack of energy and exhaustion. It never occurred to me I could stop, and I don't think that leading the race had much to do with this desire to keep moving forward. I was sufficiently ahead of second place that the race was mine, but it still seemed surreal and in a way I didn't believe it enough to have it fuel my forward momentum. It wasn't my *why*.

Luckily, I never had to find out what the consequences of either decision would have been when running on empty. At the top of the cliff, there was a gentleman with a spare energy gel, and three years later I still remember how good that blueberry sugar rush tasted. It was all I needed to dive off the platform, swim to the other side of the lake, jog to the transition area, and refuel. A few servings of oatmeal and one peanut butter and jelly sandwich later, off I went on to my last, victory lap.

Just under three hours later (my first lap was 35 minutes, but I was mostly walking by the end), I crossed the finish line as the World's Toughest Mudder Champion 2017, a female winner of the 24-hour obstacle course race (OCR). Final placing is determined based on the highest number of completed 5-mile laps with just over 20 obstacles. Some of the obstacles have to be completed before you can move on; others have a running penalty for failure. Penalty obstacles require you to run a penalty that doesn't count toward your final racing mileage, and can add up to 2.5 additional miles of running with each "5-mile" lap. I covered 90 official miles or 18 laps, but with countless obstacle failures due to the upper body fatigue, I ran over 110 miles that weekend – about 90 more than on any of my runs that year and over twice as many as what I've ever done on a single run. I started this race as a dark horse – it was my first endurance OCR race, a challenge I gifted myself as a reward for a successful season of racing. I had no goal beyond hoping to move uninterrupted for the duration of the race.

Twenty-four hours doesn't seem long enough to change a person, but there's something about the intensity of the experience and the effort it requires that means it does. I finished the race a different person, but not because of winning, or matching the female distance record, or being the first person ever to win the first lap and the overall race. The true reward was far more subtle, something I didn't appreciate until months after the race: it made me realize that I don't really know where my performance limits lie. It made me question my preconceived notions of "too far", "too hard" and "I haven't trained enough for that". It made me want to push harder to find them, and it took away the fear of the unknown. It helped me find my *why*, the one that kept me going for those 24 hours but that I couldn't identify before: because I can, and because I want to know just how far I can go.

I wasn't nervous coming into this race, despite having no clue whether or not my body could handle the challenge. I was grateful even to be able to consider running 100 miles a possibility – less than ten years ago I was struggling to do just one.

———

I grew up as a gymnast, spending my childhood years in the gym. I loved the sport so much that it wasn't just a part of my life – it *was* my life. Being good at it made it easy to spend hours each day in the gym, travelling around Europe to meets on the weekends, and thinking about training on the rare occasion I was doing something else. After years on the Slovenian national gymnastics team, at the age of 17 my career came to a screeching halt. It was the year I could qualify for the Olympics, my one and only childhood dream at the time. I'd been struggling for some time by then with mental blocks where I would lose muscle memory of a certain trick or simply change my mind and stop mid-air, usually resulting in a crash. But it was manageable, and good days were good enough to keep my dream alive.

A week before the qualifying meet we did one last dry run at our local gym. My routines were good and I did well. My coach told me to take the day off afterward, but I wouldn't listen, and something happened that day I still can't fully understand. It was like a full software and hardware crash in my brain. I lost all of my muscle memory of the past 11 years and while the day before I was doing double pikes on the floor, now I could no longer figure out how to do a handstand. Perhaps I pushed myself too hard; perhaps I fell one too many times; perhaps my brain decided to protect my body because I wouldn't. What I thought was a temporary struggle ended up being the breaking point, and I never competed again after that day in the gym when I was supposed to stay at home.

I not only lost my dream of competing in the Olympics, but my life also changed in an instant. I spent most of my days in the gym, and all of my friends were there too. I was at a sports high school where everyone knew me as a gymnast. All of that was gone in a day. I had to redefine myself, find out what I wanted in life, and how to fill those 40 hours per week I now didn't spend in the gym.

In the couple of years that followed, I almost doubled my weight in my mission to eat all of the ice cream and chocolate I never had growing up. I went from being an athlete to the point where running a mile caused my calves to cramp. I struggled with eating disorders. I partied and drank. I kept making promises to myself of things I would change starting tomorrow, promises I knew I couldn't keep. After graduating high school I moved to the United States for college. I wasn't sure what drove me overseas, but looking back I think it was my escape – I needed to get away from the life that reminded me every day of the past and what could have been, and moving to the other side of the world seemed like it could be far enough away. It was the right decision to make: the new environment helped me get my life back on track, and once I accepted I wouldn't get back to where I was at 17 in a day, things slowly started to change for the better.

Ten years later I'm probably in the best shape of my life, back as a full-time athlete living the dream I had as a child. I can't pinpoint the day when my life changed again, perhaps because coming back was a lot harder than letting myself go. Perhaps because the journey back was so gradual I stopped noticing the small changes that ended up changing my life. I just took life one day at a time. I got back into fitness one run at a time, and I returned to healthy eating one meal at a time. I accepted the days when I didn't stick to the plan and celebrated those when I did. I'm grateful for those years of struggle. I know I never want to let my fitness slip because being able to go on any kind of adventure means more than anything to me, and exploring the outdoors is what brings me true happiness in life. But perhaps the most important lesson I learned was that it's OK to lose everything. There was a time when I thought I could never devote myself to one passion to the extent it takes over my life, but the truth is that doing that makes me feel alive and I don't know how to do it any differently once I find something I'm truly passionate about. And that's OK, because I know, even if it doesn't work out, even if I lose it all, if I have to start all over again from scratch, I'll eventually be OK. And I would know I really gave it my all.

How do you train for a 24-hour race? I had no clue. Additionally, I decided to do this race only a couple of months before the event so even if I'd had a plan there'd have been little time to execute it. I showed up in Las Vegas in November with a suitcase full of gear to hopefully get me through the fluctuating temperatures in the desert, and hoped that years of running under my belt would give me enough of a base to make it through most of the race, then I'd somehow survive the rest. Although I hadn't done a run longer than 15 miles in over two years, I had been running 8–10 miles daily for almost four years by then, not skipping a single day of working out. I had a handful of zero running days due to injuries, but I'd found ways to cross-train through those as well. Over the past year I'd put in an hour of strength training specific to the sport per day and completed over 40 obstacle course races, hitting the podium for over 30 of those and winning 17. I also knew I loved the long-distance running, something I picked up when I moved to the US, slowly building my mileage up over the years. I knew my chances for doing well were good, but I had no idea what exactly "good" would mean.

Because my decision to race was last minute, I didn't officially qualify for the elite contender heat: the front-of-the-line starting position with the transition area close to the race course, and the eligibility to win distance-based podium bonuses. I was thus starting with the hundreds of other runners, lining up in the starting corral 2 hours before the race to be as close to the front as I could get. When the gun went off I had no idea where I was relative to the rest of the female field, knowing that all of the elite racers were already ahead. I also didn't know how to pace for this race, so I figured I'd just go comfortably fast until I could no longer move. That way, once the wheels fell off, I'd be in a good spot and potentially finish the race in a respectable place. Unknowingly, my comfortably fast pace put me up front, and I finished the first 5-mile lap, also called the sprint lap, in first place. This was worrying: no one has ever won the sprint lap and continued on for the rest of the race in the lead, and I was thinking to myself I probably started a bit too fast. Everyone else had the same thought, and I kept hearing advice to slow down from my pit crew and racing friends. Stubborn as I am, I didn't listen.

Obstacles opened in a rolling fashion; at the start, we were running past them. This stretched out the crowds so we never had to wait in lines, and gave me the opportunity to familiarize myself with the loop and find a routine. We started each lap from the tent village – the transition area where our crew of up to four people helped us to fuel, change gear, switch shoes, treat blisters and anything else that needed fixing during the race. Some people took a break in the middle of the night to catch a nap in their tent; some of us fighting for the top spots never stopped moving. I wanted to minimize time spent in the transition area, and took most of my fuel to go, eating the last bites while jogging up the first hill. After a few hundred yards, the obstacles started, and for the rest of the 5-mile lap we alternated between running and scaling obstacles: lake swims, monkey bars, monkey rings, rope climbs, tall walls to get over, mud pits, rolling under barbed wire, a 40-foot cliff dive, ice-water dunk and more. Each lap had up to 25 obstacles (not all were opened all night), 15 of which included some form of water submersion.

The sun went down around 6 p.m., and I was still running comfortably fast. Not fast enough, however, to generate enough body heat to stay warm, and I quickly realized I'd need to change into a wetsuit to avoid hypothermia while crossing over ten water obstacles each lap. Never having practised that before, the wetsuit change was a disaster, and I had to repeat it three times to get it right – first I forgot to take my running shorts off, and the second time I put it on backward. After almost an hour of fiddling with the gear, I was certain I had lost the lead. But having run almost 50 miles already (or ten laps), I had a sufficiently large lead and combined with others having to add neoprene to their outfits as well (albeit likely much faster than me), no one passed me – so I kept on running comfortably fast. Later in the night my wetsuit got too warm, so I asked a friend who was helping athletes in the transition area to cut it at the calves with a knife, all without taking it off, while I was busy eating a peanut butter and jelly sandwich. Then I got cold and we duct-taped the holes back together. Digestion issues leading to diarrhoea right before sunrise caused some unpleasant accidents that made me ditch the neoprene altogether at 4 a.m. and shiver through the remaining 8 hours of the race.

Oddly enough, I fell in love with these problems of the race; it was the first time I had enough time to screw up *and* fix my mistakes. It's still what draws me to endurance OCR – no matter how prepared you are, things will go wrong. It's exciting to know that those problems don't mean your race is over; rather, they give you the opportunity to troubleshoot, adapt, and do things you never expected to do.

Throughout, I kept on running comfortably fast, motivated by trying to keep warm. I was shocked – I never expected to feel this good this late in the race, and I think everyone around me – racers, my support crew and race management – was in a similar disbelief. Sure, my knees and ankles ached, I had long ago changed into the comfiest shoes I'd brought with me, I needed help from fellow competitors to make it over the walls since I could no longer fully lift one of my arms (and help at these events is allowed and encouraged), and most of the grip-intensive obstacles defaulted to running the penalty loops rather than making it across the obstacle successfully. The wheels were shaky but they hadn't fallen off yet.

My support crew was tracking the leader board posted in the transition area village so I knew where my competition was relative to my position. We all wore timing chips and there were several timing mats on the course; we always knew where the other competitors were and how many laps they had already completed. This way I knew if I had some extra time to eat a bit more between laps, and whether or not I had to go faster, or if I could slow down out on the course. My lead started to increase, and eventually I lapped the second-place female, putting myself into an over-two-hour lead. It was around that time when I started to think I might be able to win this race. But with hours left in the race, I didn't want to let those thoughts talk too loudly in my head because I didn't want to be disappointed. It's much scarier having a placing goal in mind compared to just doing your best. Instead, I focused on the moment, trying to interact with as many people on the course as I could, dividing each lap into smaller, more manageable segments. To the top of that hill, over those obstacles, across that lake.

I loved the atmosphere; at night, everyone's headlamps and colourful strobe lights made the course light up like a holiday village. During the sunrise the sound of the bagpipes, a sunrise tradition at this race, and the return of the daylight sent shivers down my spine. Wearing my leader bib earned me cheers and encouragements that kept me going more than any fitness preparation could. So I kept moving. One foot in front of the other, refusing to stop.

Just like my journey back to being an athlete, I'm not entirely sure when my race went from "I'm just having fun here" to "winning the race". After doing a few more of those long races I've learned that your body can go only as far as your mind is willing to push it, and everything starts to hurt when you decide you are done. My wheels never came off, but the last lap was probably the hardest thing I'd done in my life by that point – knowing it was almost over, all of the pain I'd blocked out in my head rushed in like a runaway train, and most of the victory miles ended up being a countdown to letting myself finally stop.

Nonetheless, all of that went away as I was nearing the finish line. The course was set in a way that the spectators in the finish arena could see you jump off the 40-foot cliff, swim across the lake, then run along on the side of the course for the last 200 yards or so to the finish line. I'll never forget the feeling of jumping over that cliff for one last time, knowing I'd win the race, hearing the cheers along the final stretch of the run, then crossing the finish line. It was a combination of exhaustion, accomplishment, pride, disbelief and pure happiness that I can never feel in anything else but these extreme physical efforts. I broke down in tears of joy.

Since that first 24-hour race, I've done my fair share of endurance OCR races, standing undefeated at any OCR race longer than 30 miles. Running the World's Toughest Mudder for the second time in 2018 was a completely different experience due to a change in venue to Atlanta and sub-freezing temperatures throughout the night, and having done it once before almost made it harder since I knew how much it hurt. But I also knew I was tougher than the course, and knowing just how much more I can give after I think I've given it my all is a solace when everything is starting to hurt.

My experience is always different, but there are elements that stay. Things always go wrong in unexpected ways and I learn something new about myself I could never discover outside of these events. There's always so much love and support from the community either on the course or on the sidelines. Finish-line tears never leave me, along with the feeling of indescribable happiness. Most importantly, no matter the length or the difficulty of the race, I always feel like I couldn't have gone a step further. I love that for two reasons: first, it means I've done my best, my one and only goal for any race I do in life. Second, it makes me wonder where my limits are. It makes me want to seek the next challenge that's even harder, even longer – something new to set my brain to and hope my body follows along until I reach the finish line.

When I quit gymnastics my coach told me, "Whatever you do in life, be the best at it." I didn't want to take his advice to heart because I didn't want the pressure to perform, especially at the time, when just getting through the day was a struggle. During those years of finding my way, all I wanted was just to be average and go through life unnoticed. I lost my competitive side and while I was never unhappy, I never laughed out loud from the joy of adventure and I never cried the tears of happiness from success. Finding my passion again in endurance OCR brought back my desire to win, albeit changed – I no longer want to beat others, but rather I want to beat the previous version of myself.

So here are my words that I live by each day, each and every race, and everything else I do in between: "Whatever you do in life, do your best at it." And do it with a smile.

IN THE FACE
OF FEAR

RICKIE COTTER

Having had a turbulent childhood, without going to school or university, you could say that **Rickie Cotter** has not trodden a traditional path. At first, navigating adulthood was tricky: work and survival got in the way of dreams and ambition. But on a positive note, Rickie was left with the ability to just get things done. She has been a painter and decorator for a long time, and now works for herself. She lives in a small flat in a lovely village with an old camper van and many bikes and pairs of running shoes. She may be low on assets, but she is rich in memories.

Rickie picks a journey that she'd like to do, and works like crazy to actualize her dreams. Cycling and running give her breathing space, and she loves the freedom they bring. She says, "You see, sometimes people's lives are not scripted. I believe you can achieve anything you want with a bit of hard work!"

Fear: an unpleasant emotion caused by the threat of danger, pain or harm.

Fear, if it were to take a form, would be a man(woman?)-eating beast. It would crawl out of the darkness and snatch your very being away from you. It freezes you in your tracks, draws the breath from your lungs and tosses your mind into a jumbling chaos of white noise. A cloak of paralyzing fear, a silent killer, your monster.

It's frightening to be afraid, yet to square up to the heavyweight that is fear is exactly how we grow. Some are more drawn to the fight than others. It comes in many forms – the battle, that is.

I remember the first night that Fear came tapping on my shoulder, clutching my guts in its fist.

It was dark and cold, and I had ridden my bike too far from home. I felt the dark night curling in around me. Simply, I was scared. Eventually, I managed to persuade myself to knock on a farm door to ask to sleep under the barn. I had envisaged that an axe-wielding murderer would answer the door and discard my remains to the pigs and sell my bike on eBay. Irrational fear. As the door slowly creaked open, after what felt like an age, a sweet old lady appeared on the other side. After I had explained what had happened, she tossed me a set of keys and said, "Dear, go and help yourself to the caravan at the end of the field."

I'd stepped into the ring for a round with Fear and punched it square on the nose, and here I was – in a spiderweb-infested caravan, eating a tin of beans that were circa 1999 – feeling, at last, like I might just survive the night.

The next morning, as I pedalled off, homeward bound, I chuckled at the fact that 12 hours earlier I was – in my head – embroiled in a catastrophe of biblical proportion. Silly, really.

It got me thinking.

What if I could build a relationship with fear? An understanding. Could I go a full 12 rounds in the ring? Where is my boundary with fear? Is it, perhaps, a moveable boundary? Surely I can't slay this beast, but maybe I could work it out with him, or maybe transform our relationship. Maybe, just maybe, we could be friends.

So, first, I'll need to go and meet him again.

―――――

There is something about the night that stirs up our imagination. Every rustle of a leaf, crack of a branch or whistle of wind spikes our thoughts into torturing plots of drama. Ironically, *we* are usually the thing to be feared. Imagine being an animal heading along your usual track, gently trodden over time by your herd, down to your usual watering hole at the edge of a river. But something isn't right – you can smell something strange. As far as that animal is concerned, you, inside your sleeping bag, are a giant, down-feathered, snoring predator, and it will either steal your food or hightail it in the complete opposite direction. My point being that if you're sleeping in a bivvy bag in the woods, up a mountain or in a cave full of bats (I would know) then it's highly likely *you* are the frightening beast – an anomaly in someone else's world.

I've been robustly testing this theory and it hasn't always been as clear cut. The next two scenarios could be deemed quite dangerous, depending on how you filter fear or depending on your level of tolerance. I learned from the first, which equipped me for the second, but the story could have ended up a darker one had my own fear not protected me.

―――――

Fight or Flight?

As my ambitions grew, I pedalled further. Curiosity drew me to the French Alps. My grand plan was to ride from Geneva to Nice via any mountain I could find. It was as fantastic as you could possibly dream of and I arrived in Nice in a euphoric, crusty, saddle-sore blaze of glory with a dry, solid baguette tied in a carrier bag to my handlebars. I was awaiting the arrival of some friends who were due in the next day. *What a wonderful night on the beach I shall have.* As the night wore on, it began to get raucous on the beach. Out of the pitch-black horizon, a boat ran aground straight on to the beach, full of drunk French men. I was beckoned over by a group of women to join the banquet they had spread out on the beach (as a hungry cyclist, this was a golden ticket), which later the drunk sailors joined. All this happened in French. I'm from Wales – we don't tend to speak much French in the valleys! Gestures, smiles and charades go a long way when there is a language barrier. The night went on and my energy waned. I took myself off into the night to a darker, quiet part of the beach. I drifted off quickly.

Something didn't feel right. I could smell cigarette smoke. My eyes bolted open. Towering over me was a man, rifling through my bike bags. I had no time for a thought process – I just fought. Hell hath no fury like a 5-foot Welsh woman. I picked up a stone and ran at the man, my bare feet pounding the hard stones, my heart thundering in my chest, screaming at him. As he ran he dropped my belongings, which consisted of a stinky pair of Lycra shorts and a dry bag with a noodle-encrusted stove. The chase wasn't about the stuff – it was automatic. I was fighting to find safety.

That night I learned I'd made a poor decision on a place to sleep. I've never made that mistake since – apart from the time I pitched my tent in the dark on a golf course in New Zealand, or when I slept in an apple orchard with automatic sprinklers. But, most of all, that night I learned that I am a fighter, that I can trust my instinct, that I can react in the face of danger, which is fear's catalyst.

Fear prepares you for danger – it's the alarm. *Sharpen up – something's coming. Switch on – we need to be alert here.*

––––––

Once, I had to descend a mountain late into the night in Kyrgyzstan. I set up the tent in a field of long, dry grass just off the dirt road I was on. I hadn't seen a car in hours and deemed it safe enough. As I began to drift off into an exhausted sleep, I heard two sets of feet running hurriedly through the grass. By the weight and speed I knew it was men, not boys. *Shit, my bike's outside.* I had a split second to make my move. Adrenalin flooded my system. Fear was here – I recognized it and it was priming me. My first weapon to be wielded was words.

I stepped out of that tent like a giant. Immediately I felt I had the measure of these two. As they shouted at me in Russian I could see fear in them. We gestured with our hands and I managed to establish they had crashed their car. As it was cold, dark and very late, being stuck halfway down a 3,000-metre mountain with no kit had manifested a sense of panic within them which had created an urgency to get off the mountain and to the nearest settlement, or even a shepherd's yurt, for warmth.

I micro-analyzed everything: their body language, tone, which one was weaker, which hand they used to point the direction (a clue to which was their lead arm, as every human strikes first with their lead arm). I adjusted my position to an awkward angle, I rotated slightly so that if I needed to push the first one he would fall over my bike (which lay behind him), giving me enough time to create a one-on-one with the weaker man, giving me a fighting chance.

My fear was giving me a fighting chance.

They needed a phone. The last thing I was going to do was get out my phone. I felt remarkably calm. I gestured for them to wait while I went into the tent. I picked out my knife... and a Snickers.

I was in control. We sat, smoked and snacked, and they became calmer. My tone and body language were slow, gentle. I was easing their fears. From our gestures I'd established that they'd crashed their car, which accounted for their look of panic (clearly it wasn't because I was an actual giant).

As quickly as they came, they left into the night. A thought crossed my mind to move to a more secure location, but I felt like the threat was neutralized. I had a fitful sleep as my body and mind struggled to switch off. I replayed the scenario, not allowing my mind to think the worst. Strangely, I felt empowered and strengthened, but before the sun rose I felt the need for movement. Moving is peaceful for me; overanalyzing is a waste of precious energy. I packed up and pedalled on as if nothing had ever happened.

———

These are both examples of fearful reactions to external threats, but what happens when we choose to expose ourselves to danger, when we seek that higher state of function that only comes when we are under pressure, exposed?

For me, I find it in the wilderness, where beauty and danger dance hand in hand, flanked only by Mother Nature and her fickle weather patterns. The unpredictable nature of travelling through the mountains is a draw to many. It's a pure test – it's as simple as survival.

Choosing Fear

During one of my first (and wettest) long-distance bike-packing races in the Scottish Highlands, my naivety put me in a position where I thought I was going to drown. Water. Life's blood flow, the fluid that keeps us and the world alive. We cannot be without it, and yet it only takes a pinch in a river, a faster flow, a hidden rock, for it to become a swift executioner. No matter how strong you are, water can take you and not give you back, forever. Knowing all this, I stood at the loch's shores in the remote Fisherfield area of the Highlands of Scotland with rain beating down on my face. I chose to try to cross.

I'm in a race. I can't stay here. My logic was being scrambled by fear.

I triple-checked my remote GPS tracker then put it down my bra and undid my rucksack.

The scene in front of me felt vast, a wide stretch of icy water.

I stepped in as the wind whipped up the surface water, obscuring my vision. My bike teetered above me, my shoulders burning like fire and shaking with the load. I was gripped.

The water rose above my knees, creeping up my thighs. It felt like it was pulling me down. Each step, I checked with my foot for any holes. A fall here would be really bad. I could feel my heart inside my head, my fragile breath leaving a final cloud of warm air in front of me.

Now the water was clutching at my waist, my tyres dangerously close to the surface of the water.

Breathe, just fucking breathe.

I considered turning back, but it was too late: I was in, and the only way out was forward.

Time was running out, my shoulders failing me. I zoned in on the shore. "I can't quit now. Come on, come on!" I shouted aloud. It made it real. I was frightened. I got angry. I was angry at myself. I'd gone too far. "You put yourself here. Get it done, Rickie."

The water peaked at the bottom of my bra and for a brief moment I wondered how I'd explain to my bike sponsors that I'd left a £2,000 bike at the bottom of the loch. I thought about how stupid it was to leave the ones I loved without a goodbye, one last cuddle.

Miraculously, the water began to recede and I heaved my sodden body back on to the shore. I lay looking at the sky with the rain on my skin and I breathed out the familiar warm cloud of air. Not my last breath after all.

I began to move again and a bizarre thing happened. I was high – high on survival. I'd gone toe to toe with the heavyweight that is Fear a full 12 rounds, and he'd tapped out. Ding ding! I'd gone from the clutches of fear to on top of the world in the space of a few life-long minutes.

———

Fear, you have many faces. I'm OK with you now. I understand my version of you. Let's keep working together. I know you have my back. I may not like you sometimes and I know you're always here. Like in any good relationship, I'll push my luck with you. We will learn a little more about one another as time goes by. But when it's time that we fight no more, make me fearless.

LEARNING TO
BE TOUGH
SARAH OUTEN

A few weeks after her 21st birthday, **Sarah Outen** stood with her hand on her father's coffin and told the gathered congregation at his funeral that she would row solo across the Indian Ocean in his memory. It was her way to get through grief. Three years later she rowed into the record books as the first woman to row that ocean solo. It was her first major expedition, and Sarah describes it as mind-blowing and empowering – for she had survived both the ocean and those first years of the grief road and seen how huge journeys can be possible, and had been captivated by life on the deep ocean. Out of that journey came her London2London: Via the World expedition – an audacious bid to row, cycle and kayak around the northern hemisphere over two and a half years, sharing the stories of the journey and fundraising for charity. Four and a half years after setting off, she returned home from an epic adventure, which she has written about in her latest book *Dare to Do* and in her recent feature film *Home*. In coming home, Sarah has had another arduous and rewarding journey of rebalancing her health and finding healing in mind and body. She is training to be a psychotherapist and lives in Oxfordshire with her wife Lucy and three donkeys.

Find out more about Sarah at:
W: sarahoutenhome.com
T: @sarahouten

My fists wrung snaking knots in my lap. Part choking something and part clinging on desperately to an edge – my hands shaped a story that my words, stuck inside and wrapped in fear and shame, could not.

"Where's your belief gone?" my therapist asked.

Crashing into my ribs, my heart was beating me up to the tune of the self-battering rants blaring out over my internal loud speaker.

"I don't know," I said, nails digging into my fingers. "I don't feel like myself right now," I stuttered, falling tears shining down my face. Too afraid to say out loud that I was on the edge of my will to be in this world. Desperate and feeling alone.

"Hey, hey," my therapist said, softly, drawing her chair in. "Look at me. Look at me." And I did, briefly. "You are going to be OK," she said, rhythmically pulling a part of me into the edge of stillness with her calm authority. "This is all going to pass. It has been shit and it's going to be shit for a while yet. But it's going to pass. You're going to feel different one day. And you're going to be OK."

A voice inside my head shouted about how she didn't know and how I was really in fact the shittest of humans and blah blah BLAH!

As though she knew what the self-destruct radio was doing, she cut me short with her own tale of crisis. If only in that tiny moment, I felt a thread of connection. Someone had heard and understood.

"I believe in you, Sarah, even if you don't believe in yourself right now."

More tears fell and my head squeezed. In opening the window into myself just a crack, I had inched millimetres away from the shadows and toward the bravest years of my life.

———

I grew up in a family that didn't do sharing vulnerable emotions and at age eight I went to boarding school for four years; by the time of this breakdown at 26 I had become something of a lone wolf when it came to asking for help. I pushed the tricky stuff down as best I could, trying to figure it out myself. When my dad died suddenly when I was 21, I lost myself in doing things and pushing on toward goals as I always had done. Doing, doing, doing. Just keep going, Outen. My attempts at expressing my pain always felt like they hadn't gone well, due to my inability to articulate or even ask for help. Or sometimes I just wasn't heard.

Six years later I found myself in a similar position. Crisis. PTSD rioting again. Self-destruction. Fear. Shame. Paranoia. Tears. So many tears. Adrenaline 24/7. Brain fog. Flashbacks. Words gone. Disconnected from myself and the world. My wife Lucy cradled me through the dark hours, holding my hand through the days. "This is our problem – we're going to solve this together." I wasn't alone, I wasn't alone, I wasn't alone. Head on her chest as we lay in bed at night, I felt calmer. I wasn't alone.

Waking up in the morning, fists clenched, teeth clenched, soaked in sweat, heart racing, I felt utterly alone. Lucy left early for work each morning.

She laid out breakfast and left me a tiny list to complete when I eventually made it down the stairs, a teary, paranoid mess, so unsure of myself that I didn't know what to do or how to do it.

Get outside.

Eat.

Have a drink.

Cycle to the farm.

The PTSD was rooted in my experience of a tropical storm in 2011, 700 miles out to sea in a tiny rowing boat by myself. After three terrifying days of being strapped to my bunk while the storm hammered violently, throwing my boat *Gulliver* about, capsizing us relentlessly, I was picked up by the Japan Coast Guard as so much damage had been wrought on the boat and its systems. I had to leave my boat *Gulliver* at sea. That rowing attempt on the Pacific Ocean was a part of my London2London: Via the World journey – a two-and-a-half-year attempt to row, cycle and kayak a loop of the northern hemisphere. I went back out to the Pacific the following year with a new boat, *Happy Socks*, and ended up diverting to Alaska due to poor weather hampering my progress. Ultimately it took me four and a half years to get back to London and complete my journey.

What I only learned later on, as I came to read and understand more about trauma and its effects, and as I explored my own ways of being and connection alongside various therapies to try and heal, was that there was layer upon layer of grief and loss woven in among the tropical storm and other life-threatening ocean moments I had experienced. Our bodies remember. And if we don't – or can't – express ourselves, then it piles up, increasing in pressure, leaking or exploding out.

In that 2018 crisis I was sat beneath a tree on a heathland with the psychotherapist I was working with, unable to articulate what was going on inside. Once again, words stuck inside, tethered by shame and pain and fear. "You don't have to do this by yourself," said my therapist, her kind frustration clear. I was paralyzed though. It was all I could do to just sit there.

And that's where Wisdom came in. My favourite oak tree. A few weeks on, I was still struggling desperately and my therapist made me promise that I wouldn't kill myself. I couldn't give her the six months she requested, but, leaning against Wisdom, my arms wrapped around her trunk and pressing into the uneven ridges of her bark, I promised three.

By degrees, over the next 18 months I came to dare more in expressing my pain and needs and connecting with others, both in and out of painful times. I was learning to let go. I painted, I danced, I hugged trees and meditated, I did some equine therapy, and Lucy and I eventually got our own little herd of donkeys.

When the PTSD rendered me unable to work on the film we were making of my London2London journey, my film-making teammate Jen let it be OK that we shifted the short-term film goal to one side and encouraged me to "trust the mess". She made it feel as safe as it could for me not to feel safe. And for me to be whatever version of myself needed to be expressed in that moment. Trust the mess, trust the mess, trust the mess – I repeated it over and over and over to myself.

What came out in therapy, dreaming and expression, was that all those younger versions of myself – on some level at least – still felt alone and threatened or unable to ask for help, through childhood to present day. Even when I hadn't been alone it was as though I had been out to sea, metaphorically.

That year, able to express myself more freely than ever before, and let go of past ways of being and pain, I came to understand the price I had paid in being a lone wolf and pushing so relentlessly all those years. I had been ill by varying degrees for a few years, even if I didn't accept the gravitas of it. I bled almost continuously for three years with a chunky uterine fibroid. My hair fell out. My immune system attacked itself, causing severe allergies, asthma and chronic eczema. I suffered a concussion when a tree branch fell on my head, and was forced into stillness and quiet. "It took a branch falling from the sky to make you stop!" laughed someone. "You don't know how to rest, do you?" said another. I had the fibroid removed by the equivalent of a C-section and the wound got infected, pinning me into stillness again, and I wrangled with frustration. It was as though my body had been shouting at me for so long to pause and rest, let go and heal. Metaphorically, the fibroid's removal represented a letting go – of past traumas and pain, past ways of being that no longer served me. I made a ceremony to mark this letting go and becoming Sarah 2.0. Sarah who knew how to pause. How to express myself in all colours of my emotions. How to dare and connect more. How to be vulnerable and lean on others. How to be a soft rock to myself.

For all my childhood I watched my father's body succumb to the debilitating grind of rheumatoid arthritis, instilling in me a sense of gratitude for my body and health. However, now I see that I had a warped view of how best to use that health. I always saw it as a call to live so fully and fast that I ran it ragged, always pushing on. Always sure that it would keep carrying me onward. Every hour was filled; sleep went by the wayside in favour of completing whatever the current goal was and I never rested. I said yes to everything, filling my time with projects and sports, and chasing my journey goals in preparation – seeking sponsors, planning, sorting and training. I couldn't hear my body screaming at me to stop and rest. After my Pacific Ocean row in 2013, I came home and was diagnosed with pneumonia and a host of severe allergies, the knock-on effects of which were really serious. And yet I didn't postpone the next leg of the journey until I was strong again, I just ploughed right back into it a few months later. Looking back, that seems reckless.

I now see that my body and health are so very precious and that I need to honour my body and needs. Was I afraid? Is that why I pushed so hard? Yes, I probably was. Afraid, I now understand, of being truly real. Of feeling and welcoming the full spread of feelings that being human brings with it, in all its messiness and marvellousness. Afraid of letting go and succumbing to the dark stuff. Afraid of expressing it. Afraid of connecting over it. Afraid of asking for others to be alongside me in it.

The introjects from my childhood about being tough seemed to be centred around being stoic, not giving up, resilience and pushing to achieve. While there's truth in all those things, I think there was an important shade of the puzzle that I was missing – perhaps the most important of all. That there is strength in vulnerability. That being tough is also about gentleness, softness and kindness. That there is empowerment in sharing vulnerabilities. And that lending our strength to others in their dark times is one of the greatest, most human ways of connecting.

So perhaps you have read to the end of this piece wondering where the adventure or the wild is. It isn't the piece that I thought was going to find its way on to the page when

I wandered round ideas of what to write. But, in fact, I have always felt that adventures are about connection and daring, albeit my traditional view was that it was a solitary quest and one where fears were stuffed down to be tamed alone. I would say that my learning to express and connect in vulnerable times has been my greatest and most perilous, daring journey of all. And the most empowering.

IT'S JUST ROUND THE CORNER

VEDANGI KULKARNI

Vedangi Kulkarni is a 21-year-old adventurer and endurance cyclist. In 2018, she rode 29,000 kilometres around the world in 159 days, becoming the youngest woman to have circumnavigated the world (she was 19 when she started and 20 when she finished). She has also cycled across the Himalayas and explored many parts of India and Europe on her bicycle. Her solo travel experiences have shown her some rather gnarly sides of the world – from being mugged at knifepoint to being chased by a bear, from being invited to sleep for the night in a random Russian truck over a few shots of vodka to being given 2 kilograms of grapes by random strangers in the middle of Canada – and yet, she absolutely loves it!

She is passionate about storytelling, mountaineering, interviewing high achievers for her personal and professional projects, and expedition management and leadership. Most of all, she is always itching for an adventure (and a box of grapes and lychees).

She recently dropped out of university to start her own business into adventure and expedition management. She hopes to provide sustainable adventure travel solutions along with several other adventure-relevant services.

Find out more about Vedangi at:
I/F/T: @wheelsandwords

On 17 July 2018, I left from Australia to attempt a world record for being the fastest and youngest woman to circumnavigate the world on a bicycle. While most of my ride was solo and unsupported, some of the bits were captured by a film crew who saw me a few times at pre-planned locations. As with all of my expeditions, not everything went to plan.

Here's an account of three of the toughest sections of the ride and how the "mind over matter" aspect of endurance activities came into play for me.

I will get a world record!

Vancouver, mid-August 2018

Flying into Vancouver from Auckland, I was well aware that time would, inevitably, be wasted. Any other day it wouldn't have mattered, but on that particular day – when my body was running on adrenaline and I was a couple of glasses of wine toward the end of the flight – I wanted to get on my bike and get going. Instead, I had to wait for the two people involved in filming my journey through the Canadian Rockies. While I waited, I went mountain biking with the team at Anthill Films, along with some people who'd flown in from far and wide to be a part of this annual event that I just so happened to be able to be there for. I'd love to say it wasn't that bad and how I perfectly fitted in to the clan of Canadian mountain bikers and people carrying cameras with lenses longer than my water bottle. But all it did was make me realize that I was an outsider – and climbing a mountain on the lowest gear of a mountain bike, wheeling unintentionally and with cadence at which I wasn't used to pedalling, I was embarrassing myself in front of the people who had thrown a lot of money at getting the film equipment sent across the pond and setting up the whole thing. It didn't help that the Canadian mountains were raging with the worst forest fires that the country had seen for a while.

I ignored everything that felt wrong with my body, forgot that I had the rest of the world to ride around and just gave the long, steep uphill everything that I'd got. At that point, I had my reputation as a cyclist to – for want of a better word – save. At the end of that climb, I enjoyed a barbecue with a few important people in the mountain-biking world, but it was at the expense of breathing in the smoke from the forest fires, which later resulted in a minor lung infection.

The film crew – Callum and Dan – arrived on separate days. The day I was due to start from the Atlantic end of Canada, I felt and looked ill. Breathing felt like a task. My head felt like someone was inside jamming on a drum kit and my eyes were burning. I had a fever, the first sign of the body fighting against any infection. I only had 120 kilometres to ride that day, but if I have to be honest, I wasn't sure if I was going to pull it off. From Squamish, there's a consistent climb all the way to Whistler – the Mecca of the mountain-biking world.

Every pedal reminded me of the fact that I couldn't breathe properly. Eventually, I reached Whistler and rushed to a pharmacy. I was told that if I continued riding at that pace, I might develop the lungs of someone who had been a chain-smoker for the past ten years. I shuddered to the thought of it, but got some medicine to get the fever down anyway.

For all that was suggested by the pharmacist, I wasn't going to stop doing what I do. I'm quite stubborn like that. "If I've set out to get a world record, I *will* get a world record," I thought to myself.

I continued that ride till Pemberton, but decided to stay there for the night as I found myself really struggling.

The next day I collapsed near Lake Joffre after crying in front of the camera and taking 6 hours to do a 37-kilometre climb. "Who on earth came up with this idea of going around the world?", I yelled at the camera, "I don't think I can do this any more. I feel so shit!"

Along the way, I walked, I stopped, I sat, I lay flat on the ground and my body refused to comply with the only task it had been set. Reaching the top, I simply couldn't stand up and move.

When I lay down on the floor next to the film crew's car, I remember thinking, "This is it! I suppose they were right. Maybe I haven't got it in me."

Fast-forward to around a week later, when the film crew was gone, I was out of the mountains and out of the smoke, doing my target distance of 200 miles per day, if not more. My lungs were fine when I was out of the smoke, but they played up again when I cycled halfway across Russia three months later in ridiculous temperatures.

In the moments when I felt weak then, I just reminded myself of how well I had done the day before and that I *had* got it in me. It was just the moments of doubt that I had to get through – and once through I'd be just fine.

Here's the thing about strength. You never know you've got it in you, until you've pushed past that arbitrary limit that you think you have.

Carry on!
Spain, toward the beginning of October 2018
"Don't panic, be still!" said the nurse as the machine conducted a CT scan on me.

I didn't remember where I was or why I was stuck to the goddamned bed, but one thing was for sure, the race was over. I was no longer going to be able to be the fastest woman to pedal the planet. I was shivering, but deep inside I knew I was safe inside the hospital.

"Take a deep breath, V, you've got this!" I said to myself. Things were blurry. I couldn't focus. My memory seemed to go on and off. My reflexes were slow and I kept throwing up. What was even wrong with me? I'd soon find out that I was concussed.

Later that day, I was taken back to the motel – a dark and dusty place next to the gas station where I had managed to push my bike, only vaguely remembering the direction of travel.

How did I even get here?

It was the day before, when I was riding late in the evening and a motorbike kept overtaking me, slowing down and then stopping, waiting for me to pass. There were two people on it and I could only vaguely see the number plate.

A few minutes later, they were next to me and one of them said something in Spanish that I couldn't understand. The next thing I knew I was pushed off of my bike, with my things sprawling over the road. One of the men held my hands behind my back and pressed a knife against my neck. I didn't move or say anything. I didn't want to be killed. Courage, for me, in that moment, was to hold myself together and look for clues. I squinted to look at the number plate and tried to figure out how the men looked – did they resemble someone famous who I could compare them with? What facial features stood out? I kept calm, while I saw the other man taking my cash. Soon after, the man holding me hit me so that I fell to the ground and then pushed me off the corner of the road so I fell into a ditch (at least that's what it felt like). There was a thud when something landed on me – it was my bike, Cappuccino. I don't remember much about what happened between then and when, a few hours later, I walked to a gas station and was taken to that hospital by kind strangers. It's amazing how many times I've found myself in tight spots and an absolute angel of a stranger has helped me out!

Concussion really does mess with your head. Over the next few days, I found myself crying at the side of the road every few kilometres, with my daily mileage halved. It was mind-boggling and heartbreaking, but for all that mattered, I was alive!

I wasn't particularly meant to be riding after the trauma I had experienced. I was told not to ride by not only the doctors but also my sponsors. But, to me, riding my bike gave me a sense of purpose, it gave my restlessness a much-needed release and I felt completely free. I knew if I had quit after that incident, I would regret it. Reckless indeed, but keeping up with my round-the-world aim and being stubborn about riding my bike was what kept me sane.

I was hallucinating and I kept feeling tired. It wasn't a surprise given that I couldn't keep much food down.

I played "Carry On" by Nate Ruess countless times to budge myself to keep going.

I informed the police and the Indian embassy in Madrid about the incident, once I finally arrived there, but never held any hope of that going anywhere. I have a theory – in life, if something's going hellishly wrong, I should deal with it as it is showing logic over emotions. Once the moment has passed, I like to think of it as a "bad moment" gone and not overthink it any further. And that's why I didn't particularly "seek justice". I just thought of it as a bad moment gone and focused on the bigger picture, which was to actually get around the world, for which I had to keep riding!

The only way out is through

Sweden, toward the end of October 2018

It was five in the morning when my alarm went off. The sleeping bag was cosy and, for a change, my body felt a perfect temperature – not so cold that I'd have to hug my dry bag with cycling clothes in tight enough and not so warm that I'd have to get an arm out of the sleeping bag to regulate the temperature. It was eerily quiet and dark.

Having camped right next to the road for so long, I was quite used to the noise. All the sounds just blended into each other, making it seem natural to my ears.

Slowly, while still in the sleeping bag, I shuffled into my cycling shorts, jersey and jacket.

You see, when everything hurts and all you want to do is sleep some more, the fact that you're in the middle of nowhere and the only way to get anywhere is by riding your bike there becomes the motivation.

This particular assumption, which has also turned out to be a reality, has been the reason for some of my questionable route choices, during my round-the-world expedition or otherwise!

When I was all set to leave, it was cold and I felt sluggish, as one usually does in the early hours of the morning. I was still suffering from the consequences of concussion from the incident in Spain. But I had to go. I had to get that ferry to Finland so that I could see a familiar face and feel at home at the home of one of my closest friends, Manu Rönkkö.

Having known him for more than three years, Manu has been an amazing support system for me. The day I started riding again after the incident in Spain, I broke down at the side of the road and spoke with him for 2 hours, describing what had happened to me, how hard it was to keep going and how bad I wanted to just stop. He suggested that he was in Finland for certain dates and if I was able to ride to his house in time, I might be able to catch up with him. Another thing he said, which played a poignant part in keeping my spirits up was, "If there's anyone I know who can get through this and get to the finish line in spite of all the difficulties, then it's you. You've got this. You've got something to prove."

That was enough for me to give it everything I had to get to Finland as fast as I could with my broken body. I was going to have to stop in Finland for up to a week to reapply for my Russian visa anyway and seeing Manu would've been like a cherry on the top.

"It's just round the corner," I kept telling myself. Fooling my brain to believe in what my mind did was the only way to get around this. Whether 100 kilometres or 10,000 kilometres, it was my mantra. Every kilometre was well earned. With the increasing pain and discomfort, I was forced to remind myself of what Abdullah Zeinab, an endurance cyclist who filmed the initial few days of my round-the-world journey, had written on the top tube of my bike, "The only way out is through!" These were the moments I completely believed in those words.

I did whatever it took to keep going – drank coffee; spoke for god-knows-how-many hours with my Belgian friend Camille – who was in Ireland at the time – about the most random things in the world; dreamed of my next adventure; indulged in endless snacking on the go; listened to audiobooks or music and everything else that I knew would keep me entertained. When you've been on the go and on your own for so long, you become aware of a lot more about yourself and your body. Being quite imaginative, I have always found it easy to find interest in and be fascinated by my surroundings. Especially when I'm outside: everything from the shape of trees to the colour of the leaves; from the lines on the road to the material it was built from; from finding places to make a camp to spotting things to make my own shelter – it's easy to be fascinated!

Eventually, I reached Stockholm, from where I was supposed to take a ferry across to Finland. While waiting at McDonald's, I messaged Manu that I was less than a day away from seeing him, which was quite a surprise for him as I hadn't been in touch to update him on my location. To prove to myself how far I could push myself, I didn't tell anybody how far I was planning on riding per day in between Belgium and Finland. I wanted to get rid of outsider expectations or suggestions and surprise myself with what I was capable of if I gave it 110 per cent.

In my head, the calculation was easy: take a ferry the same evening, get across to Finland in 9–10 hours and ride the final 200 kilometres to the bike shop owned by Manu's mum's partner, Sakke. However, I looked at my phone again and realized I only had 7 minutes to board the ferry (instead of the 1 hour 7 minutes I was prepared for!) and I was an 11-minute ride away. The next ferry wouldn't be until the next day and Manu wouldn't be around then, so I absolutely had to take that ferry.

I like to think of myself as a calm and composed person in a panicky situation, but in that moment of realization, I was anything but that.

I sprinted to the ferry, hoping and praying that it would somehow be delayed. It wasn't.

I got there with 2 minutes left to go. I had to urge the guys at the entrance of the ferry to let me in. I think I had tears in my eyes. I was shaking.

Eventually, I was let in after I showed my ticket. The people at the gate weren't pleased with me, but I can only hope they realized that I had no choice. I tried to sleep for the majority of the ferry ride across the Baltic.

Once in Finland, I apologized to the men at the gate and wrote them a thank-you note for their patience. I had 200 kilometres to go, which is equivalent to 8 hours of riding on a good day.

Needless to say, I wasn't having one of them. With a puncture and several missed turns along the way, it took me between 12–13 hours to get to Helsinki. "Mind over matter," I had been telling myself all the way. As long as I was moving forward and moving fast, I would get where I wanted to go. I willed myself on and kept positive as much as I could.

By the time I got to Velobia, the bike shop where I was supposed to meet Manu, he was standing outside.

He gave me a big hug, told me that he was proud of me and knew I could do it, and gave me a punnet of black sable grapes. Traditionally, that's what good friends do. They help you push yourself to your limits and then give you what they know you'd crave the most after that – great company and sweet grapes!

Soon after, we went to a climbing gym where I did my worst bouldering session of all time. It was never a great idea to go climbing after the ride anyway, but the fact that I'd be in Finland until I got my new Russian visa and would get to rest my body in between those days meant that I could use the adrenaline I had from seeing a best friend after months toward bouldering and tire myself out even further.

I'd be lying if I said that I wasn't proud of myself. As of that moment I reached the bike shop, I had ridden 22,000 kilometres around the world. I could comfortably say that I "only" had 7,000 kilometres more to ride until I got to the finish. I think it was then that I believed in my capabilities the most and knew that the finish was just round the corner. I had never felt so broken, yet so strong.

What lay ahead was a wintery ride across Russia and a mentally draining ride across India, but that's a story for another day!

Eventually, I did get around the world. I was almost two months late to my finish line from my initial attempt of doing it in 100 days, but expeditions don't always go to plan. Plans change, people back out from the team at the last minute, routes change, weather changes and everything can go against you if you're in for a bit of bad luck. That was the case with me getting mugged at knifepoint in Spain, getting chased by a grizzly in Canada and being stalked by strangers in Australia, facing several health and mechanical issues and being faced by the big "F" – failure! But the more I think about the things that went wrong, the more I realize that perhaps I should give more importance to the things that went right. To the road angels who saved my life in several situations and strangers who didn't know me yet decided to be kind to me. It was the kind strangers who left a mark on my heart rather than the horrendous incidents that almost killed me. And that has played such a huge part in my love for the outdoors! If there's anything that I've learnt from the expeditions and adventures that I've been on so far, it is to trust – to trust the people, to trust nature and to trust myself!

ACKNOWLEDGEMENTS

I'd like to thank, from the bottom of my heart, all of these incredible people who believed in this book and helped to make it a reality. Working on this project was a dream come true for me, and I couldn't have done it without you.

Aliénor le Gouvello ◆ Ann Daniels

Anna McNuff ◆ Annie Lloyd-Evans ◆ Anoushé Husain

Antonia Bolingbroke-Kent ◆ Beth French

Carmen Kuntz ◆ Cat Vinton ◆ Emily Chappell

Emma Svensson ◆ Ewa Kalisiewicz ◆ Hannah Maia

Jenn Hill ◆ Julie Anne Christy ◆ Kate Rawles

Misba Khan ◆ Paula Flach ◆ Rea Kolbl ◆ Rickie Cotter

Sarah Outen ◆ Vedangi Kulkarni ◆ Debbie Chapman

Marianne Thompson ◆ Lucy York

Madeleine Stevens ◆ Emily Kearns ◆ Vicki Vrint

Hamish Braid ◆ Clint MacDonald

COPYRIGHT ACKNOWLEDGEMENTS

Have you enjoyed this book?
If so, why not write a review on your favourite website?

If you're interested in finding out more about our books,
find us on Facebook at **Summersdale Publishers**
and follow us on Twitter at **@Summersdale**.

Thanks very much for buying this Summersdale book.

www.summersdale.com